Wakefield Press

The Haigh's Book of Chocolate

THE HAIGH'S BOOK OF chocolate

Cath Kerry

including recipes from leading Australian chefs

and photographs by Mick Bradley

Wakefield Press

Wakefield Press
Box 2266
Kent Town
South Australia 5071

First Published 1998

Designed by Liz Nicholson, design BITE, Adelaide
Chocolate illustrations by Beth Chandler, Adelaide
Typeset by Clinton Ellicott, MoBros, Adelaide
Printed and bound by Hyde Park Press, Adelaide

National Library of Australia
Cataloguing-in-publication entry

Kerry, Cath.
The Haigh's book of chocolate.

Includes index.
ISBN 1 86254 460 3.

1. Haigh's Ltd – History. 2. Cookery (Chocolate).
3. Chocolate. I. Title.

641.3374

Wakefield Press thanks Wirra Wirra Vineyards and Arts South Australia for their continued suport.

Chocolate Picnic

'Take on a picnic a slab of the very best, darkest, least sweet chocolate, sensibly insulated, and nuts which are fresh, let's say almonds and hazelnuts. They will still be in their shells so take a nut-cracker too. If the chocolate has no guidelines for breaking it, take, for instance, a parmesan knife to crack it with, or use the oyster knife you have brought if the picnic is in that kind of place. Take no other sweet food to this picnic, and offer, after a suitable rest, only crisp apples.'

Gay Bilson, restaurateur and writer

Con

tents

Making Chocolate

Chocolate Breakdown

Chocolate Meltdown

The Recipes

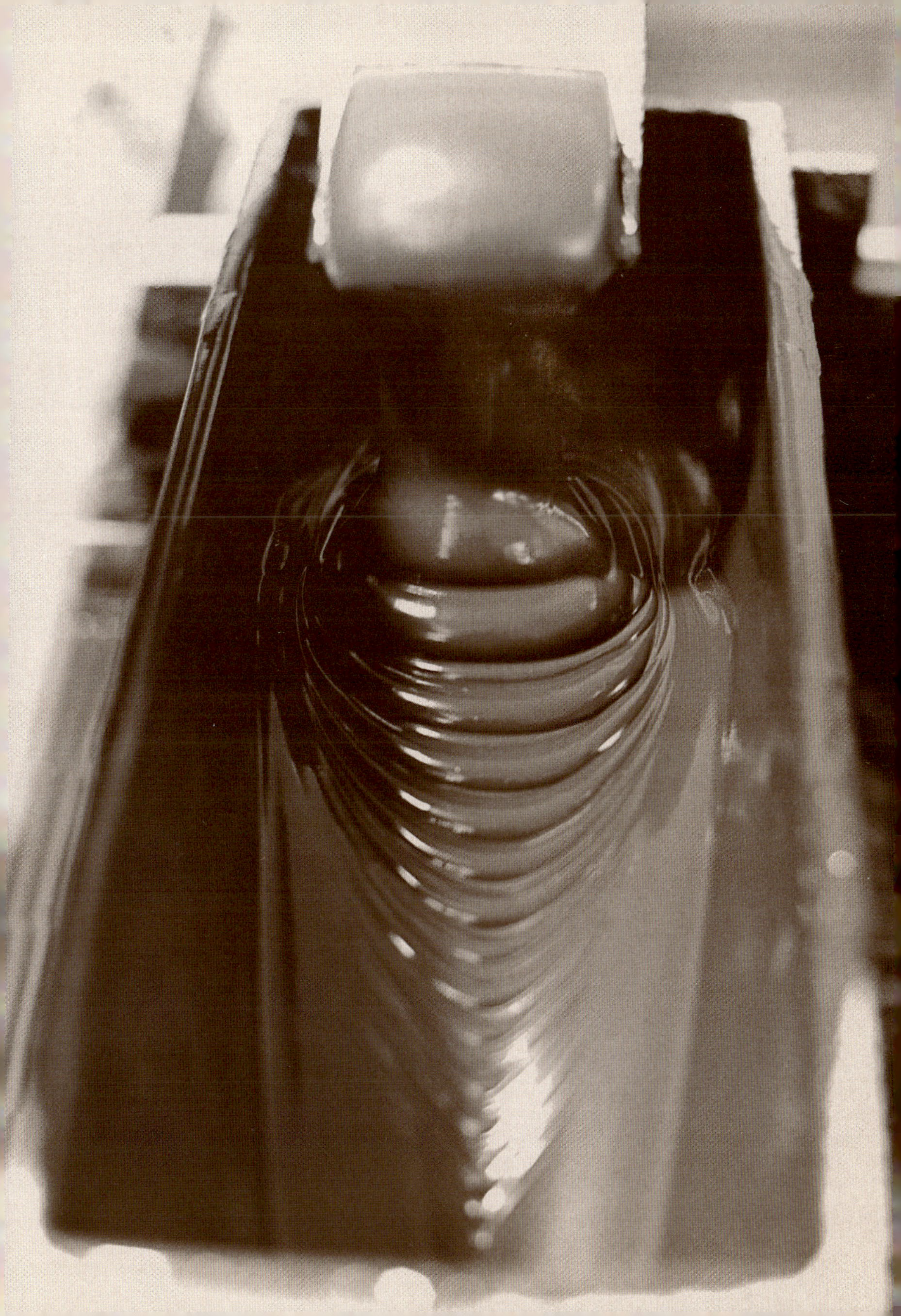

Foreword *by Alister Haigh*

Many people ask me why chocolate varies so much and what makes Haigh's products so different. Some of the answers are provided by Cath Kerry in this book. Cath tells the story of chocolate-making the Haigh's way from bean to Bilby and also provides delicious eating with a marvellous selection of recipes. Mick Bradley's photographs add to the book's allure.

As a fourth-generation manager of a family business I cannot claim to have the same confectionery skills as some of our team at Haigh's. Even the apparently routine tasks in our factory require skill, and these are now being formally recognised – hand-dipping, for instance, is now recognised in the industry as an artisan skill. Our hand-made, hand-decorated Apricot Fruits (invented by my great grandfather, Alfred) recently won champion chocolate at the Royal Melbourne Dairy Awards.

In these days of rationalisation, out-sourcing and automation, it is vital that companies like Haigh's continue the traditional methods of manufacture and ensure that these skills are recognised and not lost. It is important, also, that formal career-paths be available to people entering the confectionery industry. If this book entices just a few people to try to make a successful career in this wonderful industry, then it will have been worth the time and effort. I hope, as well, that the book in its own small way will further enhance Australia's reputation as a producer of fine foods and in particular high-quality chocolates and confectionery.

My vision for Haigh's is: 'To be recognised globally as makers of the finest chocolates.' I believe we are on the right track.

Preface *by Cath Kerry*

Chocolate is seductive. American writer Geneen Roth said, 'Chocolate is no ordinary food. It is not something you can leave, something you like only moderately. You don't *like* chocolate. You don't even *love* chocolate. Chocolate is something you have an *affair* with.'

With its complex history, sociology and psychology, chocolate is more than just a sweet. I've often felt that this very seduction, however, also detracts from the careful craft and purity inherent in good chocolate. I am not a 'chocoholic' and find the expression demeaning just as I find it ludicrous that health food shops sell a nasty chocolate substitute.

Many years ago, I became fascinated by the small chocolate house of Haigh's with its 'retro' labels and solid band of devotees of all ages. How could this company survive? What drove it to continue in the face of standardised flavours and multinational take-overs?

Food writer Cherry Ripe coined the term Culinary Cringe for her book on Australian food. Our cultural and culinary cringe makes it hard to believe that not only is Haigh's the only chocolate company in Australia but one of only a handful in the world to make chocolate directly from cocoa beans. Furthermore this hapens in 'little' Adelaide.

My curiosity or fascination coincided with the company's desire to put their own history down on record. I was in the enviable position of adding practical experience to theoretical knowledge. I was allowed to witness, in an 'up close and personal' way, the daily running of the factory with Simon Haigh and Stuart Chandler, taste the product at every stage of manufacture, question John Haigh and Alister Haigh about the family and be forced to analyse many, many chocolates. Familiarity, I am pleased to report, bred an even deeper respect and admiration for the Food of the Gods.

From the Amazon to Australia

From a Drink to a Confection

The story of chocolate is firstly the story of a beverage not a confection. Chocolate had been drunk in Central America for over three thousand years and in Europe for at least three hundred before it occurred to people to eat it. When Alfred Haigh started making chocolates in Adelaide in 1915 he embarked on an endeavour that was still in its adolescence.

The practice of drinking chocolate, coffee and tea changed European social customs in the eighteenth century and later also changed the role of wine and beer in the popular diet. Taverns were rowdy, while chocolate, coffee, and tea houses were civilised meeting places, conducive to good conversation. Wines and ale caused drunk and disorderly behaviour while the new beverages were uplifting and stimulating. All three exotic drinks became fashionable at around the same time, the late seventeenth century, and were the reward of a century of expanding European exploration, colonisation, exploitation and trade.

Coffee had been introduced to Europe through Venice and Amsterdam from the Moslem East, tea had come in from China, and chocolate via Spain from the New World, in particular Central America.

The cultivation of cocoa trees had spread from the Amazon basin through to Mexico and the drink made from the beans was drunk by an elite, often as part of a ceremony or ritual. The beans had value also as currency – archaeological digs have unearthed counterfeit beans made of clay.

On his fourth trip to this area in 1502, Christopher Columbus touched briefly at the mainland of what is now Nicaragua. The cocoa beans he brought back with him to

From Spain the fashion of taking chocolate was introduced into Italy. The grave question arose among them whether chocolate taken in the morning broke the fast in Lent. The Cardinal Branaccio battled long to prove that chocolate could not break the fast and that anyone might fast during the whole Lent as perfectly by drinking chocolate as if he had only partaken of a glass of cold water.

Alexis Soyer

(1809–1858), French writer

Spain failed to impress. Twenty years later, the Spaniard Hernan Cortes made an expedition to Mexico and conquered the Aztec communities, adding them to Spain's territories.

The chocolate drink that was introduced to Spain by Cortes in 1528 was at first just a curiosity – bitter, rich and flavoured with vanilla and another novelty, the chilli. Not until the Spaniards flavoured chocolate with sugar, and substituted softer spices such as cinnamon for chilli, did they grow to like its unique taste. They even started making it occasionally with milk rather than water!

There is no evidence that the Mayans or Aztecs used chocolate to flavour food. Europeans took to the flavour and played with it. Old Sicilian recipes show a wide use of chocolate. Spanish nuns in Mexico developed the now traditional chocolate flavoured 'mole' in what is otherwise a typical Spanish sauce. French sauces for game were finished with chocolate in a manner that seems alien to such a 'reasoned' cuisine.

Chocolate-drinking gradually spread to the rest of Europe through the Spanish territories of the Netherlands, Naples and Sicily. Unlike coffee and tea, it was known to be nourishing. The Catholic clergy praised it as an aid to piety. As a beverage, it technically did not constitute a break in fasting, and fashion-conscious or greedy worshippers could even have chocolate brought to them during the service.

The growth of European sugar consumption also helped popularise the new trio of bitter beverages, but chocolate remained frozen in the image of status symbol. Of the three, it was the most time-consuming to prepare – as preparation required servants. While tea and coffee enlivened the mind, chocolate's stimulating effect was not as acute – rather, it fed the body. Drinking chocolate came to be seen as a ritual associated with luxury, indulgence and idleness.

What was this chocolate drink like? Tea and coffee are infusions, where boiling water extracts a flavoured essence from the roasted bean or fermented leaf. The liquid is drunk while the solids are left behind. On the other hand, when cocoa beans were ground and mixed with a liquid, generally water, they were included as part of the drink. The rich cocoa butter would rise to the surface if the beverage was not properly prepared. To prevent this the chocolate was not only whipped vigorously with a special wooden wand (a molinette), but also blended with a little corn flour to help amalgamate the butter. It was thick, warm, delicious and by the nineteenth century, an anachronism.

If only there was a way to remove the cocoa butter so that a drink could be made as easily as tea. This happened around 1820 with the development of the cocoa press. Cocoa in powdered form put an end to the old tradition of chocolate-drinking but opened the door to chocolate confectionery. Sadly the drink lost its status but eating-chocolate took its place.

Eating-chocolate is still nourishing – the American company Hershey provided bars of chocolate for the American armed forces during the Second World War. Hiking rations always contain a hearty block of dark chocolate. But most importantly it remains a pleasure, a luxury, a personal reward, a confection that ignores the age barrier, that satisfies both the 'quick fix' and the need to analyse and discriminate.

What use are cartridges in battle? I always carry chocolate instead.

George Bernard Shaw,

Arms and the Man

The Beehive Corner

It flatters you for a while; it warms you for an instant; then, all of a sudden, it kindles a mortal fever in you.

Madame de Sevigne

(1620–1705), French courtesan and writer

The Beehive Corner building has always been a landmark in Adelaide, standing at the cross-roads of King William Street and Rundle Mall, the main shopping thoroughfare. The first Haigh's shop was a part of the building, not in Haigh's present position facing Rundle Mall, but around the corner at 34 King William Street.

On 1 May 1915 Alfred Ernest Haigh, great grandfather of Alister and Simon Haigh, opened for business in his new premises.

He had bought a quality sweets business named Stratmann's from Carl Stratmann, a successful but rather individual confectioner. It is alleged that Stratmann flew the German flag from his shop and in 1915, tired of the taunts and harassment, sold up and went to Melbourne to make jam.

Born in Adelaide in 1877, Alf Haigh went to school as a teenager in Jamestown in South Australia's mid-north after the death of his father in 1882. Early details of his life in the region are sketchy, but we know that he made boiled sweets in Jamestown. A clipping from a local newspaper in 1902 mentions him attending a Jamestown party with his fiancée. There is some evidence that he was involved in the manufacture of farm machinery, with a Haigh's Reaper being patented in the early 1900s. Alf worked on the Perth to Kalgoorlie pipeline as an engineer, earning enough money to move in 1905 to Mount Gambier in South Australia's south-east and open a mixed business with his new wife and baby son Claude Alfred Haigh.

Alf was an energetic entrepreneur. He introduced Mount Gambier to ice-cream and set up the first silent picture shows there. He expanded in 1912 by opening shops in nearby Pinaroo and Lameroo to sell the sweets he made

in Mount Gambier, the train line making it possible to travel between each business.

Business prospered, allowing him to return to Adelaide and buy a house in Park Terrace, now Greenhill Road, Parkside, and the Stratmann shop in the Beehive Building. With the business came equipment and Stratmann's recipe books, some of which still exist. At that time, the confectionery was made on two upper floors, sugar being taken up by pulleys.

There was competition in those days, including from some names that are now just a memory. Melbourne had Hillier's, Newman's and James Chocolates, Sydney had Alexander's and California, Adelaide had Ritz Chocolates, situated on King William Street in the next block. Alf Haigh quickly began adding his own particular flavour to the industry and in 1917 started producing the chocolate-covered fruit centres from locally grown produce that are still among the company's most popular treats.

By 1919 Alf needed to transfer the manufacturing to larger premises, and he built a small factory on a spare block behind the family house in Parkside (now the Haigh's Visitors' Centre). Chocolate confectionery became a main part of his production, with chocolate being imported from Nestlé in Switzerland.

At around this time, individual shops in the Beehive Building were being offered for sale and the Haigh's premises at number 34, strangely enough, was offered to Alf's competitor Silas Martin of Ritz Chocolates. The shop around the corner housed F. Basse & Co. Jewellers, which had been experiencing lean times. Sensing an opportunity, Alf Haigh offered the highest amount for a lease ever heard of in Adelaide. In 1922, Haigh's was now in the city's prime location, 2 Rundle Street. 'Meet me at the Beehive corner' came to automatically mean 'meet me at Haigh's'.

Chocolate is heavenly, mellow, sensual, deep, dark, sumptuous, gratifying, potent, dense, creamy, seductive, suggestive, rich, excessive, silky, smooth, luxurious, celestial. Chocolate is downfall, happiness, pleasure, love, ecstasy, fantasy . . . chocolate makes us wicked, guilty, sinful, healthy, chic, happy.

Elaine Sherman,
twentieth century American writer

The persons who habitually take chocolate are those who enjoy the most equitable and constant health and are least liable to a multitude of illnesses which spoil the enjoyment of life.

Brillat Savarin, 1825, *The Philosopher in the Kitchen*

The shop at that time was much larger than now, and fulfilled the functions of factory, retail outlet and meeting place. Various machinery was imported, including a chocolate-making plant from America. The old soda fountain is still downstairs. Cakes were sold and on a Friday night twelve 'girls' were employed as shop assistants.

John Douglas Haigh was four years old in 1933 when his grandfather Alf died suddenly. John's father Claude took over as managing director. The business had opened shops in Hindley Street, Rundle Street, beach-side Glenelg and regional centres such as Broken Hill, Gawler and Murray Bridge. By the beginning of the Second World War, however, businesses everywhere were rationalised and the Beehive Corner shop was divided to make smaller premises, concentrating on confectionery.

Supplies were difficult in the war years – sugar rationing only ceased in 1947 – but as Australia grew its own sugar it was possible to continue manufacture of boiled sweets. Haigh's made wrapped toffees for the armed forces. John Haigh remembers packing them at night with other members of the family.

The question was whether John would come into the business. He had an idea that he might do Veterinary Science, and remembers vividly the evening he was forced to consider his future seriously. On Friday evenings, before reading the till and closing the shop, Claude would meet his wife in town. John would finish sport and eat with his parents at the Maple Leaf restaurant. One evening, with John in tow, Claude was approached in the street by an acquaintance who offered him twenty thousand pounds for the whole factory and business, a large sum in those days. 'Not for the moment thanks. I'll think about it.'

Claude had a heart problem and felt that John should join him in the business at the end of the year rather than

H. MORRIS
OPTICIAN
H. MORRIS OPTICIAN
KEEP TO LEFT
HAIGH'S CHOCOLATE DEPOT
HAIGH'S
HAIGH'S CHOCOLATE DEPOT

Day before yesterday I took some chocolate to digest my dinner, in order to sup well, and I took some yesterday to be well fed so I could fast until evening. This is what I find agreeable about it, that it acts as you intend it to do.

Madame de Sévigné, 1671, in a letter to her daughter

go to university. The company was there if John wanted it; he just had to hurry up and make up his mind. John thought about it, and realised that the chocolate business was not a bad way to make a living!

When he came into Haigh's, John soon found that the company was making poor quality products under great difficulties. The two existing confectioners were capable but guarded their knowledge jealously. They had good confectionery skills but knew little about chocolate, and the equipment they had was inadequate.

After Alf died the factory had been held together by factory manager Harold Lewis. He had been an apprentice with the Haigh family in Mount Gambier and worked with Haigh's for fifty years. He is still remembered for his loyalty and hard work, but he was not a confectioner. John realised that he was not going to learn much in the family factory. The confectioners saw him as a threat and no one else in Australia would train him.

'I always had a desire to make the best. You're born that way. I like to eat the best and I wanted to make the best,' he says.

Who made the best chocolate in the world? The Swiss. John would try to go to Switzerland.

The Swiss Connection

There are many Swiss chocolate pioneers whose names still signify 'chocolate', names like Tobler, Cailler, Peter, Suchard and Lindt. The reputation of the Swiss in the chocolate world rests not only on their product, but on two inventions without which chocolate would not be what we love today.

Daniel Peter married into the Cailler family in 1863 and

worked on a way of combining milk, another Swiss national product, with chocolate. Chocolate and moisture don't mix well and not until Nestlé found a way, in the 1850s, to condense milk, and then further reduce it to powder, was it possible to combine the two successfully for taste and texture.

Milk chocolate not only further opened the public's tastebuds to chocolate but also gave the confection a wholesomeness that could be exploited. It was now good for children! Manufacturers in other countries were quick to take up milk as an ingredient and chocolate would soon overtake all other sweets in popularity.

Joseph Lindt worked on a way of making eating-chocolate smoother. In 1879 he developed the machine called a conche – it was shaped like a deep shell. Heavy rollers moved slowly back and forth, grinding and aerating the chocolate. This gave chocolate its final sophistication in texture, and finished and refined the flavour. Joseph Lindt's company eventually became Lindt and Sprungli, still makers of the finest chocolate.

In the first part of the nineteenth century, eating-chocolate was still a novelty and a brown slab could look very unappealing in a sweets shop competing with bright jewels like pastel-coloured fondants, barley sugar sticks and other boiled sweets.

At the age of nineteen, John Haigh contacted the Swiss Consulate and wrote to Switzerland's top ten chocolate-makers. Seven didn't reply, two refused and one, Lindt and Sprungli, accepted him for the simple reason that they wanted an English-speaking boy to be a companion for their director's friend's son, who was to train there in 1950.

John remembers this invitation as the turning point in his life, and he maintains a close relationship with the Lindt company and the families he met. He needed to absorb everything and Lindt and Sprungli allowed him free reign, placing him in a different department of the factory each month. John would write up his notebooks each evening.

Lindt and Sprungli's generosity was endless. Not only did he learn about the machinery Haigh's would need and how to operate it, but also how to find the best quality ingredients. John learnt where Haigh's Adelaide operation was taking too little care, how their beans were just not good enough, how to distinguish a good raw ingredient.

It was a delightful existence for a young Australian in 1950. John Haigh's eyes close dreamily at the mention of Lindt's milk chocolate bar Lindor. 'I was there when they invented it. It was so delicate that it took a long time to get the moulding right. It kept breaking and we could eat all the experiments. They got it right in the end, of course.

'It was made with *cream*, not milk.' I stand corrected. 'With cream.'

Apparently the only poor products that the Swiss made were their fondants. There was no national liking for delights like Peppermint Creams. But John Haigh believes that the Swiss were mistaken. If they had made their creams like Haigh's do, they may have liked them. But then again, he went to Switzerland to learn about chocolate rather than centres.

Before coming home, John spent time in America, looking not only at production methods, but also at shop styles and marketing.

He became managing director in 1959 when his father became immersed in his thoroughbred breeding enterprise. Improvements were ongoing and important new machinery was gradually installed; the factory was enlarged and modernised. Haigh's was now able more easily to produce quality chocolate Easter Eggs, for instance. By 1958 a high-speed refiner from Germany replaced old chocolate roller mills and there was new roasting equipment. The company's ability to invest in equipment was due in large part to income derived from contracts to supply bulk chocolate to South Australian confectioners Hoadley's and Amscol for some lines.

New equipment and methods helped keep the retail prices of Haigh's own products reasonable, as did the company's practice of selling chocolates exclusively through its own outlets. By operating its own shops, Haigh's was able – and still is – to control the conditions in which the chocolates are stored and presented, as well as the quality of service.

Haigh's also operated the concessions – with cordials, sweets and chocolates – for the Clifford Greater Union Theatre Circuit, opening in the Piccadilly, North Adelaide, in June 1954. From 1960 Haigh's also had the concessions for the Majestic Theatre (now Her Majesty's Theatre) and other cinemas such as the State, West and Sturt theatres. Foyers were glamorous entrance halls where you could sit or meet friends – only tickets were sold there, not confectionery. At interval, people thronged to the front of the stage or screen to buy refreshments. A 'tray boy' would materialise just before the lights went up, carrying a pale blue tray with 'Haigh's' written on the front, a strap around his neck. Chocolate-coated fruits and nuts were ideal for cinemas, as were gift-boxes of special chocolates. Cordial drinks and chocolate-covered ice-creams were already staples of the cinema.

Haigh's Aprichocs, too good to roll down the aisle!!

Television became cheap and popular during the 1960s, leading to a temporary decline in the cinema's popularity. Cinema managements decided to use their own staff to sell refreshments. In response, John took the bold step of opening shops in Melbourne; to ensure safe delivery of the chocolates, the company ran its own trucks.

From that time Haigh's has continued to consolidate its operations carefully. The company has recently focused on upgrading its equipment to increase capacity. There is now

a retail outlet in the flagship position of the Block Arcade in Melbourne. Haigh's 'livery' has been standardised, featuring shop designs that are simple and classic while still subtly reflecting the company's heritage.

Haigh's dominated awards at the 1998 Royal Melbourne Show, winning the Championship Chocolate Award – for Haigh's Apricot Fruits – and nine gold medals. It was the fifth time in six years that the company had won the championship award.

John Haigh is Chairman of the Board but sons Alister and Simon run the company, continuing the tradition of quality chocolate from quality ingredients. John Haigh eats at least five chocolates a day, has a chocolate with his cup of coffee and never walks through the factory without taking a chocolate. Alister seems to manage five or six chocolates through the course of the day and Simon is continually testing the product. They are all energetic, trim men.

Theobroma Cacao

Sourcing the Beans

Jute sacks of cocoa beans sit bunched on pallets of the Haigh's Parkside factory waiting to be processed. The variety of bean and its country of origin are stencilled on the sack – Papua New Guinea, Ecuador, Ghana and other locations kept a close secret. The beans are around two centimetres long, the size of a thick, rounded almond, dark brown, streaked or flecked with purplish black. They show little promise of the flavour they will yield.

Chocolate manufacture is now quite centralised, with large European companies in Belgium, France and the Netherlands concentrating exclusively on processing in bulk up to the cocoa liquor, cocoa butter and cocoa stage from beans shipped to them often from their own plantations. This base ingredient is sold on to industrial or specialist chocolate-makers. Confectioners large and small, catering to the mass market or to connoisseurs, can buy their chocolate processed as cocoa mass or cocoa liquor right through to 'couverture'. They are then free to finish and fashion their confectionery in their own style.

Buying in the processed base ingredient does not necessarily mean poor chocolate. So why does Haigh's continue to be one of the few remaining manufacturers in the world to begin with the raw cocoa bean to make its chocolate?

A quality product can only come from good basic ingredients and with Haigh's chocolate, this starts with the beans. It is simply a question of wanting total control over flavour and quality.

Like wine grapes, cocoa beans have different characteristics depending on variety, area of origin and processing. Simon Haigh controls the blending and processing of beans as meticulously as any fine wine-maker, using his highly developed sense of taste and smell.

It has been shown as proof positive that carefully prepared chocolate is as healthful a food as it is pleasant; that it is nourishing and easily digested ... that it is above all helpful to people who must do a great deal of mental work.

Anthelme Brillat-Savarin

(1755–1826), French magistrate and gastronome

Haigh's keeps in close contact with its agents, keeping them informed of the company's particular requirements. The agent's choice of beans depends on quality and supply. While the base bean for Haigh's chocolate comes from Ghana or the Ivory Coast, it must be balanced for acidity and depth of flavour according to how the final blend will be used. These 'flavour' beans come from Papua New Guinea, Ecuador and other countries. Plain chocolate bars need a sweeter, more delicate bean than dark 'enrobing' chocolate, which must compete in flavour with a dominant centre such as ginger or mint. Milk chocolate needs a bean that will not be overpowered by the addition of milk powder.

The pleasant task of tasting a variety of chocolate bars quickly demonstrates the reason for this attention to detail. At best, mass-produced chocolate flavour is becoming standardised. While the chocolate flavour is instantly recognised, much mass-produced chocolate is dull and flat. A satisfying chocolate has a length of flavour that is complex and lasting, whether it be milk or dark. A fine chocolate-maker needs to use specific flavour beans to suit the different chocolate confections it produces.

The Tree and its Fruit

Classified as 'Theobroma Cacao' in the eighteenth century by the botanist Linnaeus, the cocoa tree is native to Central America. Once chocolate had been introduced into Spain, it quickly cast its magic over the taste buds of Europe. Nations with colonies in the tropics established their own cocoa tree plantations in other parts of the world.

The cocoa tree can grow up to 20 degrees north and south of the equator, and technically we could grow cocoa trees in Australia. West Africa now produces the majority of the world's crop – mainly all-purpose base beans – while Central America's output is now very small but nonetheless highly esteemed. (On the other hand coffee, which is indigenous to the African continent, is now thriving in plantations in Central America and South America, such as Brazil and Guatemala.)

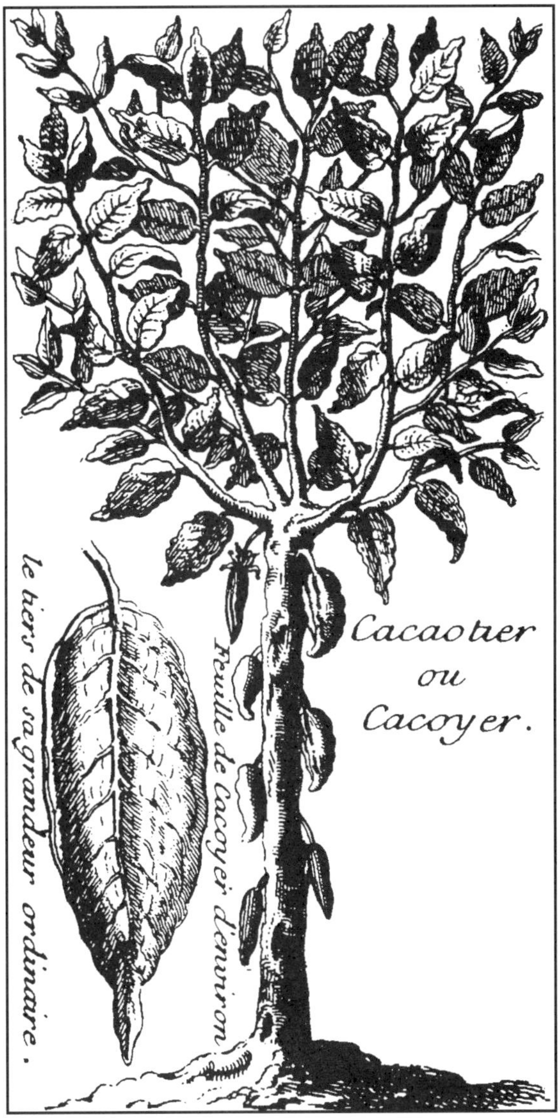

She habitually ate chocolates for their sustaining quality; they contained much nutriment in small compass, she said. They saved her from starvation . . .

Kate Chopin

(1851–1904), American writer

The cocoa tree is a small evergreen that grows naturally under the canopy of the rain forests. Cultivated for the last two thousand years, the trees need protecting from direct sun and wind and must be assured of warm, even, moist conditions. Their large leaves shelter the cocoa pods as they grow and taller 'mother' trees such as plantains and bananas are grown amongst the cocoa trees, giving shade and possibly a crop of their own. As luck would have it, the most delicate variety of cocoa tree, the Criollo, possibly the original, indigenous cocoa tree of the Amazon Basin, produces the most esteemed beans in small quantities, while the more robust Forastero is plentiful but dull.

The flowers and the resulting pods grow directly from the main trunk and branches. Early botanical artists in Europe found this quite bizarre and, when reproducing the crude sketches made by returned explorers, assumed they were mistaken. The artists' drawings have the fruit hanging from stalks like peaches or apples.

Cocoa tree flowers, which are not unlike fuschias, are small, white and abundant but have no perfume. About 50 to 100 pods will set, growing to the size of a small football, 20 centimetres long. As they ripen, they change colour to red, deep orange or yellow depending on variety. Fruit and flowers may exist at various stages of maturity all year round, although the crop is harvested twice a year for convenience. This has to be done by hand, taking care that the tree is not damaged in cutting away the pod, as the flowers and fruit appear on the same part of the trunk each season. Damp tropical conditions also make fungal infection dangerous on open cuts in the bark.

Cocoa Pod to Cocoa Beans

Cut open, the pod reveals tightly packed rows of beans that look a little like elongated lychees. They are covered in a translucent white pulp. This is sticky, juicy, acidic and slightly sweet and may have been the first part of the cocoa tree that was eaten. In parts of Central and South America a fermented alcoholic drink is still made from the cocoa pulp. The pulp can also be made into a jelly or cocoa vinegar and the outer husk can be used as animal feed or as organic compost.

The miracle is that we have chocolate at all. As with so many of our most treasured foods, a transformation has to take place before we can enjoy it. Who would eat an olive when picked straight from the tree? A fresh vanilla pod has no smell. Malting brings out the flavour in the grain that we expect in whiskey. What happy accident led to the fermenting of cocoa beans?

This most important step in the production of the chocolate flavour takes place as part of the plantation work and production. The beans are scooped out by hand. Traditionally they are placed in mounds, covered with banana leaves and allowed to sit for three to ten days, depending on the variety. While this method is still widely used, many beans are now fermented in vats or large fermentation crates where their development is easier to monitor.

The mounds are placed in full sun. During this time, the temperature of the seeds rises further due to fermentation and the sticky pulp drains off. Biochemical changes involved are complicated; it is enough to say that the beans change colour from purple to chocolate's characteristic dark brown and give off the first hint of a chocolate aroma.

Once cleaned of pulp, the beans are dried. This is still generally done in the open air by the heat of the sun. The

beans are spread out on mats or large raised drying racks, raked and turned daily. Although the sun is hot, this is tropical country and there is a continual danger of showers. The beans must be protected when rain comes, either by covering them with tarpaulins or by pulling over them a series of canopies on rollers. Beans that have taken too long to dry can become acidic, while damp beans risk attack by mildew. On large plantations, beans may be dried with electric dryers.

After inspection and grading, the beans are packed in 50 kilogram bags, to be dispatched to large manufacturers such as Lindt in Switzerland, Cadbury's in England and Callebaut in Belgium. Other beans are selected and bought by brokers who distribute to manufacturers of small-batch production, such as Bernachon in Lyon, France, or Haigh's in Adelaide, South Australia.

While cocoa is a tropical plant, its destiny lies in cooler climates. Very little chocolate production takes place where the beans are grown, apart from the initial fermentation. When the sacks of beans reach Adelaide, they are dusted of any slight remains of dried pulp before entering into their next stage of metamorphosis. Roasting will crack away the dry husk and produce something we can start to recognise as chocolate.

Making Chocolate

Several times a week, a faint but delicious aroma of roasting chocolate wafts delicately over the small leafy suburb of Parkside, on the edge of the parklands surrounding Adelaide. No one seems to mind.

The Haigh's headquarters are compact, with factory, offices and visitors' centre in a corner position bounded by Greenhill Road and Douglas Street, taking up little more space than a few suburban house blocks. Every step in the manufacture of chocolate happens here, from the grinding of the beans to the final arranging of finished chocolates in their presentation boxes.

There is even room for expansion in an area where Haighs used to make its own gift-boxes. This is no longer practical, but riffling through a back store-room you can still come across magnificent specimens from the fifties. One example, with gilded edges and full-blown roses on the lid, finished by a ribboned bow, was designed to hold a four-pound selection (yes, around two kilos) of Haigh's finest creams. What a present!

Alister Haigh, chief executive officer, bemoans the loss of some of Haigh's past treasures, innocently discarded as styles and techniques changed and space was cleared. 'Fortunately, I'm a bit of a Steptoe,' he says.

Alister has kept old labels and Easter egg moulds, but the best way to preserve the past is to continue to use it. For a small chocolate manufacturer, nothing much needs to change. Chocolate is a simple, pure product with few tricks of technology and the *mélangeur* (mixer) made in Germany, dating from 1890, is still used today.

But the most striking piece of machinery in the chocolate room, the winnower, stands next to the roaster.

I was brought up to believe that you never ate chocolate until after lunch, and even now am truly shocked at those of my friends who will eat chocolate cake for breakfast, and one who has been known to demolish half a box of the best chocolates before she even gets out of bed in the morning.

Helge Rubenstein

(b. 1929), English writer

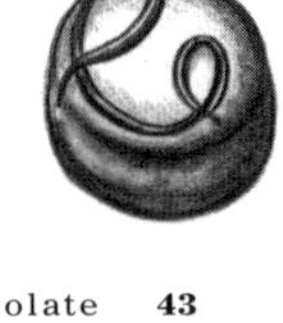

Roasting for Flavour

> I don't have to watch my figure as I never had much of one to watch. What you see before you is a lifetime of chocolate.
>
> *Katherine Hepburn*, actress

The beans are roasted at around 140 degrees in a revolving metal drum. This step is crucial to the final taste of the chocolate. With roasting, at long last the scent of chocolate fills the air.

Roasting dries out the outer husk of the bean, making it brittle enough to be easily cracked off. But the heat, more importantly, creates a useful and pleasant change in the chocolate's carbohydrates, known as the Maillard reaction (after the Frenchman who investigated it) which, grossly simplified, means that they undergo a colour change and an intensifying of flavour. This effect is what gives that special flavour to much of our food – coffee, roasted nuts, barbecued meats, brown bread crusts, dark beers and, of course, chocolate.

Over-roasting, like over-cooking, can burn the beans, while under-roasting may leave the natural bitterness and prevent the beans from developing character. Experience and a well-developed chocolate 'nose' is required for someone to recognise when different beans are roasted to perfection.

The beans then go to the winnower, a magnificent wooden structure, built as carefully as an antique side-board. Attached to a series of blow-pipes, it resembles a church organ and looks equally impressive.

Here the beans are cracked and the outer husks blown away, leaving behind the kernel. Cocoa beans have now become chocolate 'nibs'. Biting into these, you have the full chocolate flavour, unsweetened. It is like biting into a very interesting almond, and the wonder is that these delicious morsels have not been eaten as they are.

Grinding For Texture

The Aztecs ground their roasted beans on a *metate*, a small, heated, curved grinding stone with a heavy rolling pin. This simple but strenuous operation continued to be the normal method for grinding cocoa beans until the advent of mechanisation in the nineteenth century. The heavy *metate* was not generally a household item (unlike the manual coffee grinder), which might explain in part why chocolate did not reach a mass market until after the 1850s. Late in the century, there were still chocolate houses in Europe that prided themselves on using the *metate* as proof of the purity of their product. In Spain and the south of France travelling chocolate grinders hauled their *metate* from town to town to grind chocolate.

When you have breakfasted well and copiously, if you swallow a generous cup of good chocolate at the end of the meal, you will have digested everything perfectly three hours later, and you will be able to dine in comfort.

Brillat Savarin,

1825, *The Philosopher in the Kitchen*

The grinder at Haighs is the piece of machinery next in line for renewal. It is the modern version of a *metate*, grinding the beans with water to cool the gringing plates. The resultant cocoa mass or cocoa liquor pours thickly from the end of the machine. The ground nibs have become simply solid cocoa particles suspended in cocoa butter.

If allowed to set, this cocoa liquor becomes a hard cake. Lightly sweetened, this form of chocolate is still sold in Mexico. Like the Mayans and Aztecs before them, Mexicans use this chocolate to make a frothy beverage, even now preferring it to eating-chocolate. This is also the block, flavoured differently, that was used to make the drink enjoyed by the French and Spanish nobles before 1828 when Dutchman Conrad Van Houten revolutionised and democratised chocolate-drinking by separating the cocoa and cocoa butter.

Back in the chocolate room at Haigh's, the cocoa liquor is warm, dark and very bitter. It is made of around 53 per cent cocoa butter but still more will be added later.

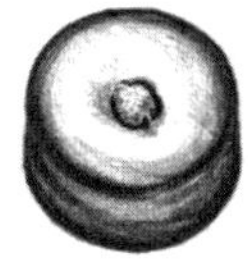

Now the cocoa liquor can go one of two ways. Ours is destined to become fine chocolate. Cocoa manufacturers, on the other hand, would put it through a hydraulic press to completely separate the butter, leaving a crumbly mass, cocoa. With the addition of a 'wetting' agent such as lecithin to help it mix with liquids, it could become drinking cocoa, or be sold to flavour ice-cream, drinks and confectionery.

Every cure of obesity must begin with these three essential precepts: discretion in eating, moderation in sleeping, and exercise on foot or on horseback. For dinner, if you must have something sweet, choose a chocolate custard . . . For breakfast, the inevitable rye bread and chocolate rather than coffee.

Brillat Savarin, 1825, *The Philosopher in the Kitchen* (On Obesity)

At Haigh's the cocoa liquor goes straight to the *mélangeur*, named after the French word 'to mix'. This is an open mixer, approximately two metres in diameter, in which granite rollers press and blend the ingredients. Icing sugar, ground on the premises to ensure purity, is added along with pure vanilla and milk powder if milk chocolate is being made.

As well as being thoroughly blended, the particles are ground to a sticky paste. The taste is there now, not just palatable but quite delicious. The English firm of Fry & Sons (now part of Cadbury's) produced the first eating-chocolate in 1847. Could this be how it tasted?

It is the 'mouth-feel', however, that needs more work. A series of vertical, water-cooled rollers take up the paste, and when it has run its course, the correct smoothness is there. This is beginning to taste in every way like the chocolate we expect.

Even here care must be taken. Smoothness equates with creaminess and lusciousness. Some of this effect comes from the cocoa butter, but it depends very much on the care taken to grind the paste to the correct consistency.

The tongue can detect very small particles. At around 50 to 70 microns the paste is still coarse. Ground finer than 15 to 25 microns, it starts to lose definition and the paste will seem too smooth. National fashion plays a part. The

Swiss and Germans prefer an extremely fine grind for a very smooth effect. Go too far, however, and the resulting chocolate can feel slimy in the mouth.

The conching machine finishes our chocolate. The piece of equipment that originally resembled a conch shell is now a large, deep barrel in which the chocolate undergoes hours of agitation. Strong, rough beating with rotating paddles gradually subsides to a gentle stirring, creating slow waves in the surface of soft chocolate. This is a delight to watch. At this stage, a small amount of lecithin, an emulsifier made from soy beans, may be added to help stabilise the mixture. But most importantly, more cocoa butter is added.

The labelling of chocolate can tell us a great deal. Only confectionery made purely with cocoa liquor and cocoa butter can rightfully be called chocolate. This precious, beautiful butter is the by-product of powdered cocoa manufacture and is in high demand. Chocolate-makers must purchase it and Alister Haigh says ruefully that his company's insistence on not compromising the cocoa butter is a major manufacturing cost.

For sophisticated kids! Fairy bread – buttered and topped with Haigh's dark or milk chocolate sprinkles and cut into triangles.

Advertising slogan

Cocoa butter's most important characteristics are that it is very stable and moves immediately from a solid to a liquid over the course of just one degree of temperature change. It melts at just below body heat. On contact with the tongue, it dissolves to allow the chocolate flavour to fill the mouth. In the same way, it will easily spread if it is rubbed on your body – so good for expensive creams, lipstick and suntan lotions.

In the conche, flavours and textures improve. Aerating the chocolate expels residual moisture and volatile acids. The flavour deepens as the disparate elements of cocoa solids, sugar and possibly milk powder homogenise in the

molten cocoa butter. Time is money, and many chocolate-makers are happy to reduce conching to a minimum. By contrast, depending on the type of chocolate being prepared, Haigh's chocolate is conched for up to 72 hours.

Chocolate is no ordinary food. It is not something you can leave, something you like only moderately. You don't *like* chocolate. You don't even *love* chocolate. Chocolate is something you have an *affair* with.

Geneen Roth, 1982, *Feeding the Hungry Heart*

Poured into holding vats and held at a molten temperature, the chocolate is ready to be poured off and used for confectionery. There are several tanks, each with their contents identified by code on the front. Couverture, which has extra cocoa butter added, will be used to cover chocolates. There are tanks of milk, tanks of dark. A chocolate lover's fantasy!

The chocolate is warm at this stage and, if allowed to set, the solid particles and cocoa butter would separate, even after all this effort. At 25 degrees the cocoa butter will start to soften and the ingredients to separate – as anyone who has left chocolate in the car on a hot day will testify.

Chocolate must be brought gently to its useable temperature with its homogenous texture intact. This is known as 'tempering' and is technically complex. To do it by hand demands a well-practised feel for the ingredients. Simply put, the temperature of the chocolate is raised and lowered, while the chocolate is stirred to prevent the formation of large cocoa butter crystals and to keep the different elements evenly distributed. Once tempered, chocolatiers can begin to create their confections.

Catering to Pleasure

There is chocolate and there are chocolates.

For a basic hit of chocolate there is the chocolate bar or tablet. This is an uncomplicated quantity of chocolate, elegant in its simplicity, dark or milk, made into blocks and conveniently divided so as to break into mouth-sized squares. These are fundamental, sensible, to be eaten on hikes for energy and comfort, to be taken on picnics, to be left on desks for thinking, to be placed inside a crusty roll for a quick snack.

Strength is the capacity to break a chocolate bar into four pieces with your own bare hands – and then eat just one of the pieces.

Judith Viorst

Chocolates, on the other hand, are confections covered with chocolate. They have long been offered as presents to show love and gratitude. Bought for oneself, they represent luxurious indulgence.

Haigh's has found over 150 different uses for chocolate. Some combinations give way when an ingredient becomes unavailable. Fashion demands the introduction of others. Some, like the Banana Cream, are retired, only to be reinstated through public demand. There are blocks studded with nuts or honeycomb; chocolate-covered fudges, nougats and mints; bars of marshmallow, marzipan and cherry; champagne-enhanced truffles ...

In particular Haigh's stays strong in two areas.

Firstly, the company took note of Australian-grown ingredients of superior quality. South Australian apricots from the Riverland are used to make the glossy Aprichocs, still widely copied. John Haigh was introduced to the little-known Buderim Ginger from Queensland, and knew it was a winner. This ginger is now accepted as the best in the world and, coated with Haigh's dark couverture chocolate, it is one of the company's most popular products.

Secondly, Haigh's perfected the chocolate-coated

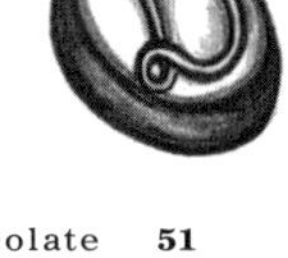

fondant cream, those chocolates that you will recognise as the soft centres of the chocolate box.

Every chocolate-loving country has its own style. The Swiss developed, perfected and prefer milk chocolate. The delicate *gianduja* is a classic filling of ground hazelnuts and chocolate, created in Italy late last century to extend the highly-taxed and therefore expensive cocoa bean. The chocolate truffle is the French favourite – chocolate softened with cream or butter, formed into irregular balls and coated with more chocolate. It was named after the elusive truffle mushroom, which it resembles in appearance and charisma.

The chocolate fondant cream is proudly Anglo-Saxon. As well as its natural fruit flavours, Haigh's maintains a long British tradition of floral scented sweets with its Rose and Violet creams topped with a crystallised flower.

The understanding of sugar and its crystalline structure, how to 'grain' a syrup or keep it clear, was a major contribution of British confectioners. Grainy, pastel-coloured sugar candies were a popular novelty as early as the seventeenth century. Finer control over the texture of sugar sweets occurred at around the same time as the development of eating-chocolate. Very soon, fondants were only seen coated in chocolate. The English firm of Joseph Fry and Sons started selling its Chocolate Cream Bar (fondant coated with dark chocolate) in 1866.

Fondant is initially soft and is shaped and hardened in starch moulds. These are shallow trays filled with an edible starch based on cornflour. Shapes – from simple rounds and ovals to more complicated shells – are pushed into the surface, creating uniform depressions. Later, the starch can be sifted and put back into the trays to start another batch. Soft fondant is poured into the moulds and allowed to set. The starch dries out the moisture, leaving the fondants firm enough to be handled. They are picked out and dusted off, ready to be coated.

A further alchemy transforms the crystallised sugar into soft velvety centres. An enzyme made from yeast is added to the fondant mixture. Once sealed from the atmosphere by its chocolate coating, the enzyme affects the structure of the sucrose or sugar, turning it liquid. How liquid it becomes depends on the amount of enzyme used and the time allowed for the product to mature. This is how a flowing centre can be coated with chocolate.

Haigh's Cherry, Apricot and Pear Liqueurs exploit this technique to the extreme. A careful bite and the 'juice' around the piece of crystallised fruit floods the mouth.

Fillings are made on the premises at Haigh's. The sweets room is like a home kitchen with giant-size 'labour-saving devices'. A few square metres of nougat are poured onto a slab, a bath of marshmallow is whipped for rocky road, someone nonchalantly pours a bottle of sparkling shiraz into the truffle mix.

Nearly thirty per cent of Haigh's chocolates are still dipped by hand. On the end of a small two-pronged fork, a truffle is dipped into a large tray of molten chocolate before being tossed into chocolate sprinkles or cocoa. While it sounds easy, coating with just enough chocolate is a skill perfected over years. The Peppermint Marrons are half coated, exactly to the top of the ridge, to maintain their sleek dark and white appearance. Roasted Almonds are double dipped, first in milk chocolate, then in dark. The skill shows too in the neatness of the procedure – there's not a drip in sight.

Much simpler than dipping is 'enrobing' (from the French *robe* for dress). Centres are placed on a small conveyor belt and passed through a slow shower of chocolate, first to coat the bottoms, then the tops. Before they reach

the end of their journey they are hand-marked with a 'squiggle' to identify the filling.

Automation also helps with moulded chocolates. Just the right amount of chocolate is poured into slowly moving moulds to make such treats as the signature pastilles and, most importantly, the frogs. A giant frog is now produced weighing in at 275 grams. A white-gloved 'keeper' lovingly wraps each one in coloured foil.

Moulds can also produce hollow shells that can be filled, then 'bottomed'. This method is fast and produces a shiny, sharp-edged chocolate. Shapes, while being well-defined and sculptural, look mass-produced. Haigh's, along with other fine chocolate-makers, prefer the softer appeal of hand-finished chocolates.

A row of polished copper vessels rotate to coat nuts and fruit centres with a chocolate of exceptional gloss. This is called panning. Chocolate is introduced at various stages as the pans turn until the correct layer of coating has been achieved. The rotation continues to round and polish the pieces. These Aprichocs, Scorched Almonds, Caramel Chocs, and Chocolate Sultanas were big sellers when Haigh's operated the concessions at Adelaide theatres and cinemas, becoming the chocolates that were 'too good to roll down the aisle'.

Chocolate Breakdown

Haigh's Haven

The scent hits you first – gentle aromas of vanilla, caramel, mocha, sweet things. Then there are the shelves, row upon row of precision-placed forms, in subtle colours of dark, amber, milk and ivory. The shops are timeless – pristine glass, gently reflecting mirrors and a hint of tradition.

Haigh's is a haven of calm, inviting you to linger, to choose. And you will.

Seasons and special occasions direct the window displays. Chocolate hearts wrapped in red speak of love on St Valentine's Day. There are boxes to celebrate Mothers' Day, Christmas and, best of all, Easter. For a chocolate house Easter is the high season. There are eggs, naturally, but it is the Bilby, the tiny marsupial with its inquisitive, sensitive nose, that has taken over as the Haigh's Easter symbol.

What do you choose? Where do you start? Chocolate-covered Coffee Hazelnut Nougat; Violet Creams, lightly scented and topped with a crystallised flower; chunky pieces of Buderim Ginger, enrobed in dark chocolate; soft fondant sandwiched between slices of Australian apricot; a whimsical peppermint frog as an afterthought; a slab of Coffee Pecan to munch in the car; Macadamias or Scorched Almonds polished with chocolate to a lacquer shine; Butter Truffles, Rum Truffles, Sparkling Shiraz Truffles.

Tasting Chocolate

Much serious thought has been devoted to the subject of chocolate: What does chocolate *mean*? Is the pursuit of chocolate a right or a privilege? Does the notion of chocolate preclude the concept of free will?

Sandra Boynton

Chocolate: The Consuming Passion

For a reasoned appreciation, it helps to know a little about the structure of chocolate brought about by melting and tempering. In addition to sugar, vanilla and possibly milk solids, chocolate is made up of solid brown particles that unfortunately do not dissolve but remain suspended in the cocoa butter. Heated, the heavier cocoa particles sink, while the cocoa butter crystals rise to the surface.

Chocolate that has been left too long in hot conditions develops a whitish bloom that is simply cocoa butter crystals. This affects the appearance more than the flavour. Chocolate stored in too moist conditions, such as in the refrigerator, becomes gritty through the sugar dissolving and recrystallising on the surface. Chocolate spoilt in this way can be used for cooking, but it makes for poor eating.

The process of tempering – raising and lowering the temperature, stirring constantly – is necessary to stabilise the cocoa particles in the cocoa butter. Chocolate that is tempered will have a cool, dry surface and will keep its shape and texture for months in the right conditions. It will break with a distinctive snap. Untempered chocolate will never fully harden and will have a dull surface.

What could be more enjoyable than really getting to know your chocolate? Wine buffs gather to 'look at' wine, the bottles hidden in brown paper, gargling the contents before spitting it out into sawdust-filled buckets. Chocolate tasting is more civilised. Furthermore, it is an ideal way for children to learn about tastes.

Firstly, have the chocolate at room temperature – chocolate should be kept in a cool place and refrigerated only in extreme heat. Be prepared to use all five senses. Try small pieces at a time and refresh the palate when necessary. Have on hand water and slices of apple.

Aroma

Allow the scents of the chocolate to seduce you for a few moments before sliding a piece in the mouth. Hunt its secrets. The chocolate should be perfumed with a hint of its accompanying vanilla, be neither too bitter nor cloyingly sweet.

Sound

You should hear the chocolate snap as you break the bar or crack when you bite.

Appearance

The surface should be shiny with no hint of streaking. When snapped, the broken surface should be craggy. This shows a high content of the crystalline, brittle cocoa butter and careful technique. While milk chocolate should still have good colour and depth, dark chocolate should be richly coloured with a hint of mahogany.

Touch

Cocoa butter is solid at 33 degrees and melts at 34 degrees. This means that good chocolate with a high cocoa butter content will feel dry and cool at first touch but will begin to melt almost immediately. Check this by placing a small amount in your hand, or better still on your tongue. It should leave a clean, non-greasy finish in the mouth.

As the chocolate melts, check for texture or 'mouthfeel'. The grinding and conching process should have reduced the particle size to between 15 and 25 microns. Any coarser and the chocolate will feel gritty; too fine and the tongue can no longer discern texture and the chocolate may feel slimy.

Place a small piece on your tongue and allow it to melt. You may also like to scrape it with your lower teeth and allow it to settle beneath your tongue. Chocolate has a unique taste. The flavour should be full and lingering. Check for a balance of sweet to bitter. There will be an element of fruitiness and acidity to lift the heavier flavours. Check the vanilla element. Artificial vanilla will be cloying.

If in doubt, start again.

Chocolate goes with ...

Chocolate is a substance that stands on its own. We may pick a Passionfruit Cream or a Milk Rum Fudge but it's the chocolate part we are looking for. Chocolate is not used to highlight other foods. It allows itself to mix very nicely with some flavours.

Not only in confection, but in all cooking, **think of chocolate** with nuts, especially roasted nuts such as almonds and hazelnuts.

think of chocolate with spices, especially vanilla but also cinnamon and cloves.

think of chocolate with some fruits, pears definitely, raspberries rather than strawberries. With their lower acidity, think of dried apricots, prunes and candied ginger.

think of chocolate with oranges in particular.

think of chocolate with coffee, a perfect balance of fetishes.

think of chocolate and mint, and why not sage and marjoram?

think of chocolate with more butter and cream.

In savoury food, **think of chocolate** with chilli or saffron and always a touch of sweetness to bring them together.

Cocoa, Cacao, Chocolate

In 1828 Dutchman Conrad van Houten invented a screw press that could remove the cocoa butter from the bean, leaving behind a brittle cake of what today we call cocoa. Not only did this change the drink known as chocolate, but it made possible the development of confectionery chocolate in solid form. Solid eating-chocolate is barely 130 years old. Before that chocolate was exclusively a beverage and had been drunk for perhaps 2000 years. Not surprisingly words around chocolate and cocoa can be confusing.

Carob

This eastern European tree with large flavoured pods has its own respectable pedigree. Now, however, the fruit is mainly used in a strange and futile attempt to imitate the flavour of chocolate in the misguided notion that pleasure is bad for you.

Chocolate

Once the name of the drink made from the fermented, roasted beans of the Cacao tree, 'chocolate' today more often signifies the solid confection. The word is thought to have come from the Aztec *xocoatl* (for pronunciation, think of the salamander axolotl), meaning 'bitter water'.

Chocolate Chips

Also known as 'chocolate buds', these are simply chocolate in small pieces. Be careful to check labelling as there are real chocolate chips and compound chocolate chips. To be safe, use good chocolate and chop it into small pieces with a large knife.

Cocoa

The original Mexican word for the tree and its fruit was 'Cacao'. Anglicised to cocoa, the word now signifies the unsweetened, dry powder separated from the cocoa butter when the bean is ground. It is used to make a hot drink and commercially to flavour ice-creams, toppings and confectionery. While it is the base for compound chocolate, a product that will never pass our lips, cocoa is nonetheless a perfectly acceptable ingredient.

Cocoa Butter

The marvellous fat of the cocoa bean sets hard but melts just below body temperature, which gives chocolate its sensual feel in the mouth. There is always a high demand for cocoa butter, by the cosmetic industry for lipsticks and face creams, and by fine chocolate-makers as further cocoa butter must be added to the cocoa liquor to make chocolate. Cheap confectionery uses other fats that leave a greasy coating in the mouth and a nasty aftertaste. It is possible cocoa butter is one of the 'good' fats that help fight heart disease.

Cocoa Liquor

Also called 'cocoa mass', this comes from grinding the roasted cocoa beans with a little heat. The near-black mass extruded from the machine contains the cocoa solids and approximately 51 per cent of cocoa butter. Makers of chocolate, even fine chocolate, generally buy in this liquor (also known as Neatwork). Haigh's is one of the few remaining chocolate-makers in the world to start from scratch, roasting and grinding their own beans.

Compound Chocolate

By separating the cocoa butter and the cocoa, you have a valuable product in the cocoa butter and a by-product – cocoa – that can be sold to make compound chocolate with the addition of unspeakable fats. Don't touch it and when buying chocolate, read the label.

Cooking Chocolate

This is generally dark but of indeterminate nature. 'Cooking chocolate' is a generic term for a chocolate that is seen as good enough for cooking, but lacking in finesse and balance of flavour. Good food means the best ingredients.

Couverture

Couverture has a higher cocoa butter content than a chocolate bar. It can be dark or milk and is the chocolate used by professionals for its spreading and coating properties. Couverture is what enrobes the fruit or cream centres as they travel on their conveyor belts through a flood of chocolate. There is no reason at all why you can't eat couverture. What is sold as Haigh's cooking chocolate is the premium dark couverture that the company uses for enrobing and hand-dipping.

Dark Chocolate

The connoisseur's choice should contain 50 per cent cocoa liquor. Many manufacturers now proudly announce the composition of their chocolate. Aficionados are seeking out chocolate with up to 80 per cent cocoa liquor, and hence little sweetness. While this is an interesting taste exercise, in the end a good chocolate needs a balance of bitter and sweet. Haigh's dark is around 52 per cent cocoa liquor. Dark chocolate is generally used in cooking and is more dependable than most 'cooking chocolate'.

Drinking Chocolate

The product sold under this name is a mixture of cocoa and powdered sugar. It is far better to make a hot drink using cocoa so you can control the strength and sweetness.

Ganache

This is a mixture of chocolate and butter (or cream), cooled together, then beaten until it thickens. This is the basic mixture that fills truffles. A ganache can be used to 'ice' a cake.

Hot Chocolate

Unfortunately, this is generally made with drinking chocolate, is very sweet and lacks depth, while cocoa has lost its fashionable edge. The hot drink known as chocolate is ready to be improved and revived! European cafés still serve a dark, rich chocolate, thick enough to hold up the spoon. See the recipe for the 'Richest Cup of Chocolate' to produce a drink more in keeping with the old Spanish version.

Milk Chocolate

While real chocolate-lovers seem to grow out of milk chocolate in their early teens, there are some very fine milk chocolates. Some flavours require a softer touch. Milk chocolate should contain at least 20 per cent cocoa, softened with milk solids. Haigh's milk chocolate includes 30 per cent cocoa so that flavour is not dominated by sweetness.

Theobroma Cacao

Chocolate has always been seductive. The botanical name for the cocoa tree comes from the Greek, meaning 'Food of the Gods'.

Vanilla

Vanilla has no botanical relationship with chocolate. It is simply so strongly linked with the flavour of chocolate that its absence would be quite noticeable, like a loaf of bread when the salt has been left out. It was being mixed with chocolate when Columbus and Cortes came to Central America at the beginning of the sixteenth century. It should be real vanilla, sometimes called Bourbon vanilla, not the artificial substitute, vanillin.

Vegan Chocolate

Some very nasty chocolate boasts vegan status. Milk chocolate contains milk but all other good chocolate is by definition vegan, that is all pure vegetable matter. More importantly, the list of contents of good chocolate is very simple: there is no need for artificial additives.

White Chocolate

White chocolate does not have a chocolate taste but certainly has the creaminess. This is because it is simply cocoa butter with milk solids added. While it does not contain any cocoa liquor and therefore is not technically chocolate, it is a thoroughly decent product that marries beautifully with chocolate. It deliciously demonstrates the qualities of cocoa butter. Using it in cooking is usually a little superfluous as the creaminess disappears into other flavours. As cocoa butter is expensive, make sure you *are* getting white chocolate, not a chemical compound!

HAIGH

Chocolate and You

How does your chocolate consumption rate? People in eight other countries eat more chocolate per capita than Australia's five-and-a-half kilograms per person a year. Switzerland has the highest per capita consumption at nine-and-a-half kilograms, but eating and making good chocolate is a national pastime over there. It is interesting that Brazil, possibly the birth-place of the cocoa tree and still a producer, has a consumption of just over one kilo per person annually. Brazilians continue to enjoy chocolate as a beverage rather than as a food.

Research tells us that fourteen out of ten individuals like chocolate.

Sandra Boynton,

Chocolate: The Consuming Passion

It is commonly accepted that there has to be something sinful and dangerous in anything we really enjoy. If you prefer your pleasures to be touched with danger and guilt, you may be disappointed to know that chocolate, far from being bad for you, is probably doing you good.

So called 'chocoholics' are simply people who like a lot of their favourite thing. The addictive power of chocolate is highly over-rated. It is perfectly natural to want something so utterly delicious. Perhaps a better expression would be 'chocophile' or 'chocolyte'.

Every thin woman wishes to put on flesh . . . Before eight o'clock in the morning, and in bed if necessary, drink a bowl of soup thickened with bread or noodles, but not too copious or if preferred a cup of good chocolate.

Brillat Savarin,

1825, *The Philosopher in the Kitchen (On Thinness)*

Theobromine has similar stimulating effects to caffeine. Phenylethylamine works like an amphetamine and is also identical to a substance manufactured in the brain when you are deleriously in love. Both substances occur naturally in chocolate and can help create a sense of well-being. The quantities in chocolate are too low to be dangerous. Any mood swings should more likely be attributed to the high sugar levels in poor quality chocolate, or simply to not getting what you want.

It has been easier to blame chocolate than hormone imbalance and an unhealthy life-style for migraines,

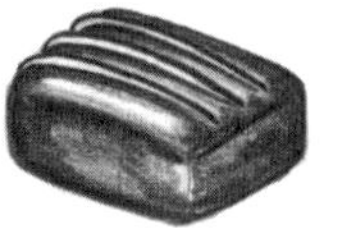

Cocoa has exhibited a significant caries-inhibitory effect when added to cariogenic diets in animal studies. The conclusion drawn is that there is a water-soluble chemical component of cocoa which shows an inhibitory effect upon total dextran synthethis of streptococcus mutans.

Vincent J Paolino,

Massachusetts Institute of Technology, 'The effect of Cocoa on Dextransucrose Activity in Streptococcus Mutans', 1978 paper presented to the International Association for Dental Research

pimples, obesity, addiction and hyperactivity. Studies are now conclusive that chocolate does not cause pimples and that other factors are more important triggers to the onset of migraines.

It is far more satisfying to have small but regular ingestions of good quality chocolate than to binge on inferior product. We are simply not active enough these days to use up all the energy from the excessive sugar and poor fats used to produce flavour in cheap chocolate.

Chocolate is a good source of magnesium, a mineral needed for serotonin, important in stabilising moods. It also contributes potassium, calcium, iron and vitamin B.

Cocoa butter, although a saturated fat, contains stearic acid. This acid has been found to elevate levels of high density lipoprotein (HLD), which lowers blood cholesterol.

While brushing teeth after eating chocolate is necessary because of the added sugar, studies in America and France have shown that cocoa may contain an antibacterial substance that inhibits tooth decay!

Chocolate is certainly not high in caffeine. A cup of coffee contains 140 milligrams of caffeine, a cup of tea 30 mg. Thirty grams of chocolate contain just 6 mg of caffeine and a cup of cocoa only 10 mg.

Are there any negatives? It is bad for dogs as it damages their central nervous system. Don't treat your pet to chocolate. Keep it for yourself.

Chocolate Meltdown

Cooking with Chocolate

Cooking will not hide poor ingredients. This is especially so for chocolate. Haigh's dark cooking chocolate is recommended in the recipes that follow. Sold to the public as Cooking Chocolate, it is in fact couverture, chocolate high in cocoa butter. It melts well and has the force of flavour (approximately 50 per cent cocoa mass) to marry with other ingredients.

I did once use chocolate with an exceptionally high cocoa mass to make a mousse, assuming that strength of flavour was everything. It was inedible. A balance of bitterness to sweetness is important.

In the end, the style of chocolate must be what you are comfortable with. Many prefer to use the gentler Haigh's milk chocolate. This will work just as well but with a softer flavour.

Some recipes need the chocolate to remain in small pieces for texture. This is achieved by grinding chopped chocolate in a food processor along with other ingredients such as almond meal. In the main, however, chocolate in cooking is used melted.

Chocolate can easily burn and should never be melted over direct heat. Melt it in a double boiler, which means simply placing a stainless steel bowl over a saucepan of simmering water. Make sure that no steam or drops of water come into contact with the chocolate or it will harden or seize up.

Chocolate can also be melted in a gentle microwave or on a plate in a low oven. Watch it carefully because, although melted, it will still hold its shape.

Good chocolate that has lost its lustre by being exposed to heat – it will be covered in a light white crust – can still be effectively melted and used in cooking.

Petits pains au chocolat – I give it here in its simplest and best form, an enriched bread or roll dough wrapped round a stick of coarse cooking chocolate, and baked in the oven until the chocolate is just about to melt. Who invented them? Certainly somebody who knew something about chocolate – and about children, and about the rightness of certain combinations.

Elizabeth David,

1977, *English Bread & Yeast Cookery*

Chocolate goes well with sex: before, during, after – it doesn't matter.

Helen Gurley Brown

Apart from an excellent truffle recipe, I have not included any recipes for hand-made chocolates. At the risk of being controversial, I believe that chocolates hand-made at home are by definition poor chocolates. The problem lies in tempering. When melted, all chocolate loses its 'temper', making it dull, matt and unstable. Generally, other fats need to be added to maintain the sheen, leading to loss of quality.

Leave chocolate-making to the experts. With over 150 varieties to choose from (at the last count), Haigh's should have enough to satisfy even the most ardent chocophile.

Chocolate for Lunch and Dinner

Chocolate can feature in every course of a dinner or lunch party. Here are three menus – the recipes are among the collection that follows.

Chocolate Dinner Party (I)

Canapes of Caponata
Pasta with Wild Mushrooms
Pork Braised with Sweet-sharp Sauce of Chocolate and Orange
Chocolate Date Meringue Cake
The Richest Cup of Chocolate with Chocolate Native Peppermint Toast

Chocolate Dinner Party (II)

Black Pepper Biscotti served with Goat's Curd
Snapper with Chocolate Red Wine Sauce
Slow Cooked Lamb with Saffron and Chocolate
Whisky Cake with Prunes
The Richest Cup of Chocolate with Spiced Chocolate Biscuits

Light Luncheon Menu

Canapes of Chocolate Tapenade
Chicken and Prawn Ragout 'Mar I Muntanya'
Gippsland Blue with Chocolate and Black Pepper Biscotti
Melon Granitas with Shaved Chocolate
The Richest cup of Chocolate with Walnut and Citrus Cake

The Recipes

Cooks must have devised more recipes using chocolate than any other food. These are a small selection that highlight chocolate's diversity. Some have been offered by Australia's best chefs, others have been in our repertoire for years and have moved into the realm of folklore. Who first devised the recipe? Where possible, recipes have been attributed to their source; others remain anonymous, belonging openly to all lovers of chocolate.

Savoury Dishes

The use of chocolate in savoury dishes was once fairly common in European countries such as Spain, France and Italy. It lost favour when chocolate came to be seen more and more as a sweet confection. We could easily revive it! The chocolate added near the end gives a mellow finish to the sauce, helps to thicken it and adds gloss.

SLOW-COOKED LAMB WITH SAFFRON AND CHOCOLATE

To serve 6

2 tbsp olive oil
1 large onion, chopped
1 medium-sized leg of lamb, trimmed of unnecessary fat
1 tsp each whole fennel seeds, freshly ground pepper and salt
½ cup raisins
½ tsp saffron stamens, soaked in 1 tbsp water
30 g dark chocolate, chopped

- Choose a heavy, lidded casserole that can be used on top of the stove and in the oven.
- Heat the oil and soften the onion.

- Add the leg of lamb, trimmed of unnecessary fat and brown a little on all sides, making sure that the onions do not burn.
- Settle the lamb comfortably on the onions and toss over the fennel, pepper, salt, raisins and saffron.
- Add enough water to cover three-quarters of the leg.
- Cover the casserole, bring the liquid just to the boil and then place in a moderate oven (180°C).
- Cook at this temperature for three-quarters of an hour, then lower the temperature to 160°C and cook a further 2½ hours. Check during the cooking time that the water has not completely evaporated. (Cooked longer, the meat will be tender, but dry.)
- Remove casserole from oven. Carefully lift lamb onto serving platter and keep warm.
- The meat should be very tender and able to be served with a spoon.
- The juices should have reduced to a rich sauce. Reduce further on top of the stove or add a little water if necessary.
- Add the chocolate in small pieces to the sauce and stir until melted.
- Pour over the lamb and serve with buttered noodles or mashed sweet potato.

CAPONATA

To serve 6 as an entree or as part of a collection of dishes.

Sicilian cooking of the Baroque period reflected its wealth by the lavish use of new and expensive ingredients. The chocolate in Caponata is now rarely mentioned. It does add a subtle depth of flavour.

1 kg eggplant, cut into cubes and salted
Olive oil for frying
2 onions
5 stalks of celery, cut into cubes
1 tbsp sugar
4 tbsp red wine vinegar
2 tbsp tomato paste
25 g dark chocolate
½ cup green olives, pitted and chopped
2 tsp capers, rinsed of salt
Chopped parsley and toasted pinenuts for garnish

- Rinse and drain the eggplant. Squeeze dry.
- Fry in olive oil (about 3 cm deep) until golden, then set aside.
- Tip off most of the oil and cook the onions and celery until soft. Add to the eggplant.
- Make the sauce in the pan by heating together the sugar, vinegar, tomato and finally the chocolate.
- Stir in the olives and capers and pour sauce over the vegetables. Garnish with chopped parsley and pinenuts.

CHOCOLATE PASTA WITH WILD MUSHROOMS

To serve 6

Make pasta (for six) from your own recipe adding a heaped tablespoon of good quality cocoa, 2 teaspoons of dark brown sugar and half a teaspoon freshly ground black pepper. Serve with the following sauce.

½ cup of dried wild mushrooms (porcini, cèpes, morels etc)
500 g fresh mushrooms, sliced
1 cup chicken stock
1 medium onion, finely chopped
1 cup cream
1 tsp redcurrant jelly
1 tbsp finely chopped parsley

- Soak the dried mushrooms for 20 minutes in water.
- Drain these mushrooms, keeping the water. Strain this through a layer of absorbent paper or a clean tea-towel.
- Rinse these mushrooms under running water to make sure there is no grit left on them.
- Simmer them in the stock and strained water for 15 minutes.
- Meanwhile, soften the onion in a little oil. Add the sliced fresh mushrooms and continue cooking a further 5 minutes.
- Add the onion and fresh mushrooms to the simmering dried mushrooms.
- Add the cream. Simmer for another 15 minutes or until the sauce has thickened lightly.
- Add the redcurrant jelly and season with salt and pepper to taste.
- Stir in the parsley.

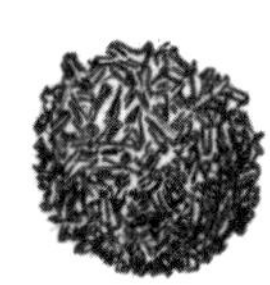

TOMATO MEAT SAUCE FOR LASAGNE

To serve 4

A traditional recipe found in a Sicilian book of the 1950s.

A little olive oil
1 onion, chopped
200 g tomato paste
250 g minced pork
30 g dark chocolate
1 tsp sugar
125 ml (½ cup) red wine
½ tsp cinnamon
Olive oil, salt and pepper
500 g lasagne

- Heat the oil in a saucepan and soften the onion.
- Add the tomato paste and cook for about 3 minutes.
- Add the pork and stir into the onion to break up the meat.
- Add the wine, sugar, cinnamon and chocolate and if necessary a little water to cover.
- Season with salt and pepper.
- Bring to the boil, then reduce the heat and simmer for half an hour.
- Meanwhile, cook the lasagne.
- Serve with the sauce.

SNAPPER WITH A RED WINE SAUCE

To serve 6 as a main course, 10 as an entrée

This recipe is based on a traditional Bordeaux recipe for lamprey eels in a sauce of leeks and red wine. Now standard published recipes for Lamproie a la Bordelaise (as with the Steak a la Bordelaise below) usually omit the chocolate. Locals however swear that at home, the sauce is always finished with a little chocolate. This recipe suits any robust, firm-fleshed fish.

2 tbsp olive oil and 2 tbsp butter
1 medium onion, chopped
1 medium carrot, chopped
1 clove of garlic, chopped
1 tbsp tomato paste
1 heaped tbsp flour
1 bay leaf, 1 sprig each of thyme and parsley
500 ml water or fish stock if available
500 ml red wine
20 to 30 g dark chocolate
3 medium leeks
250 g mushrooms, chopped
1½ kg snapper fillet

- Heat 1 tbsp of oil in a saucepan and soften the onion, carrot and garlic. Add the tomato paste and cook together for 3 minutes.
- Add the flour and cook a further 3 minutes.
- Add the bay leaf, herbs, stock and red wine. Bring to the boil, lower the heat and simmer for 10 minutes.
- Add the chocolate and stir until melted.
- Check the seasoning with salt and pepper and add more water if the sauce is too thick.
- Strain the sauce for a more elegant finish (optional).
- Keep warm for service.

- Meanwhile, clean the leeks, keeping a little of the green. Cut into rounds.
- Soften the leeks and mushrooms in 1 tbsp of butter.
- When ready to serve, lightly brown and cook the snapper pieces in the remaining butter and oil.
- Serve either on individual plates or on a serving dish. Arrange the snapper on a bed of leeks and mushrooms. Cover with sauce.

TAPENADE WITH CHOCOLATE

To serve 6 as an appetiser

200 g black olives
25 g dark chocolate
4 anchovy fillets
1 heaped tbsp capers, rinsed of salt
1 clove garlic, peeled
Handful flat parsley leaves
½ cup (approx) olive oil

- Remove stones from the olives.
- Melt the chocolate.
- Blend ingredients together, using enough olive oil to moisten the mixture.
- Mixture should be evenly chopped, blended but not too much of a paste.
- Serve on toasted croutons.

CHICKEN AND PRAWN RAGOUT 'MAR I MUNTANYA'

To serve 6

'Mar i Muntanya' means 'Sea and Mountain' and refers to the combining of meat and seafood in the same dish. As seen in Paella, this is common practice in the Catalan dishes of northern Spain.

6 chicken portions, preferably from the leg, cut in two for convenience
12 medium-sized green prawns, shell on
Olive oil for cooking
2 medium onions, chopped
2 tbsp tomato paste
½ cup white wine
1 bay leaf
2 sprigs of fresh thyme
About 4 cups water
Salt and pepper to taste
Small fist of fresh parsley
3 large cloves of garlic
½ slice bread, about 30 g
¼ cup of almonds, toasted in the oven
¼ tsp ground cinnamon
30 g dark chocolate, chopped

- In a large casserole, heat the oil and brown the chicken on all sides. Set aside on a plate.
- In the same oil, toss the prawns until they turn pink. Set aside.
- Soften the onions in the casserole for about 10 minutes then add the tomato paste and continue cooking for another 3 minutes.
- Return the chicken to the pot, add the white wine, bay leaf, thyme and just enough water to cover the chicken.

- Bring to the boil, cover, lower the heat and simmer for ½ hr or until the chicken is just tender.
- Season with salt and pepper.
- Add the prawns and continue cooking for a further 10 minutes.
- While the chicken is cooking make the 'Picada', the traditional Catalan thickening for the sauce.
- In a food processor, grind together the parsley, garlic, bread, almonds, cinnamon and chocolate, adding ½ cup of water to help it form a soft paste.
- Just before serving, stir the Picada into the sauce and simmer for 5 minutes.
- Check the seasoning before serving.

BRAISED PORK WITH A SWEET-SHARP SAUCE OF CHOCOLATE AND ORANGE

To serve 6

Another old Italian recipe, meant for long, braised dishes of hare, wild boar and even tongue! Try it with pork neck, braising beef or veal shanks.

1½ kg pork 'neck'
2 tbsp olive oil
1 medium onion, chopped
1 small stick celery, chopped
1 medium carrot, chopped
2 tbsp chopped bacon or prosciutto
Sprig of thyme
1½ tbsp flour
½ cup raisins
Salt and pepper to taste
40 g dark chocolate
¼ cup pinenuts, browned in oil
¼ cup candied orange peel and a 5 cm piece of orange peel
1 tbsp dark brown sugar
Dash red wine vinegar

- Have the pork in one piece, tied to hold its shape.
- In a heavy-bottomed casserole or braising pot, heat the oil and brown the pork on all sides. Set aside.
- Add the onion, celery, carrot, bacon and thyme to the pot and cook for 5 minutes or until the onion is translucent.
- Add the flour and cook for about 5 minutes, stirring well.
- Place the pork on the mixture, season with salt and pepper and add just enough water (or white wine and water) to half cover it.
- Simmer covered for three-quarters to 1 hr or until the meat is tender.
- Just before serving, add the rest of the ingredients except the vinegar, stir in and simmer a further 10 minutes.
- To finish the sauce, remove the meat to a serving dish and adjust the seasoning with a dash of vinegar and more salt and pepper if necessary.
- Serve the meat in neat slices, coated with or sitting on the sauce.

TURKEY (OR CHICKEN) WITH MOLE POBLANO

To serve 6

1½ kg turkey breast (or 6 chicken breasts)
¼ cup sesame seeds
Butter or lard for cooking
1 onion, chopped
3 cloves garlic, chopped
¾ cup almonds
¼ cup peanuts
3 dried ancho chillies, soaked in water or use 3 fresh chillies, to taste
1 thin slice of bread
1 tbsp raisins
½ tsp each of cloves, cinnamon, pepper, anise
Up to 2 cups chicken stock
25 g chocolate

- Toast the sesame seeds and set aside until the dish is served.
- Roast or poach the turkey or chicken while you make the sauce as follows.
- Soften the onions and garlic in lard or butter. Set aside.
- Brown the nuts in the same pan. Set aside.
- Remove seeds and membrane from chillies and 'toast' in a little more lard or butter. Set aside.
- Grind all ingredients – except the turkey or chicken, sesame seeds and chocolate – together in a food processor, using the stock to make a thick sauce.
- Heat a little lard in a saucepan and gently cook this sauce – the 'Mole' – for about 5 minutes. Add the chocolate and stir gently until melted.
- The sauce should be just thick enough to coat the meat. Add more stock if necessary.
- To serve, arrange the turkey or chicken on a serving dish and pour over the sauce. Sprinkle sesame seeds over the top.

VENISON RAGU AND DOLCE FORTE SAUCE

To serve 4

'Dolce Forte' means 'Bitter Sweet'. This recipe comes from Bill Marchetti of Marchetti's Latin Restaurant, Melbourne. Don't be tempted to use expensive cuts of meat. Topside and other prime cuts dry out during such long cooking. This is an excellent treatment for game but also works well with braising beef.

15 g dried porcini mushrooms
800 g venison, cut into 4 cm cubes
2 tbsp olive oil
2 tsp butter
100 g piece of pancetta, cut into ½ cm cubes
1 medium onion, finely chopped
1 clove garlic, finely chopped
1 chilli, seeded
½ stick of celery, finely chopped
1 medium carrot, finely chopped
200 ml white wine
2 bay leaves
100 to 150 ml meat stock
200 ml canned tomatoes, chopped
1 tbsp tomato paste
Chopped parsley
70 g pine nuts
50 g raisins
50 g dark chocolate
1 tbsp sugar
2 tsp red wine vinegar
Salt and pepper to taste

- Soak the mushrooms in water until soft. Rinse under running water to remove any dirt and chop.
- Season the meat with salt and pepper.

- In a large heavy-bottomed braising pot, heat half the butter and oil. Add a single layer of meat to brown well on all sides.
- Remove to a dish with a slotted spoon and continue with another layer of meat, adding more oil and butter if necessary. Repeat until all the meat is browned.
- The pot will now have a thick layer of browned stuck-on juices. They must never be burnt.
  This browning is very important. Without the utmost care the dish will lack flavour.
- Add the pancetta and cook over moderate heat until fairly crisp, stirring to scrape off meat juices clinging to the pot.
- Add the onion and cook until translucent, removing the last of the juices from the bottom of the pot.
- Add the garlic and chilli (unchopped)
- Add the celery, carrot and porcini mushrooms and cook until vegetables are tender.
- Add the wine, bring to the boil to cook off the alcohol.
- Add the venison and any juices that have accumulated in the bowl.
- Add the bay leaves and enough meat stock to just cover the meat. Lower the heat and simmer, semi-covered, for an hour or until the meat is tender.
- Add the chopped tomatoes, bring to a boil and add just enough tomato paste to give the dish an appetising colour.
- Add the remaining ingredients, stir well then turn off. It must not keep boiling once the these Dolce Forte ingredients have been added.
- Before serving check the seasoning. Serve with pasta, preferably Studio Marchetti Chocolate Bitter Fettucine, available in some speciality food shops.

Sweet Dishes

Dessert and cake making can be more exacting than savoury dishes; it is worth remembering some of the basics.

Baking Blind

This allows you to bake a tart case a little longer than the filling, so that it is crisp, especially the base. Line the empty, uncooked tart case with aluminium foil and fill with dry beans. This helps the pastry to hold its shape while cooking. Once out of the oven, remove the beans and foil and keep them for another time.

Baking tins

Spring-form or loose-bottomed tins allow the cake or tart to be removed without it being tipped upside-down. Unfortunately, they are not suitable for very liquid mixtures as they will leak before the mixture has set. The sides of a spring-form tin undo to release both the sides and bottom of the cake.

Butter

This is one of the great ingredients of the world, along with chocolate. There is no substitute. In most cooked dishes, sweet or savoury, it is best to use unsalted butter so you can control the salt. A pinch of salt, even in cakes, is still often added, but the salt in salted butter is usually far more than the dish really needs.

Caster sugar

Finely ground caster sugar should be used in all cakes and desserts, especially when the sugar is to be whisked with egg or creamed with butter.

Cooking times

Experienced cooks can tell if a cake is cooked by gently touching the top and testing its 'spring'. Some simply rely on their nose. When the mixture begins to smell like cake, it's close. A sure-fire method is to insert a fine skewer into the middle and check that it comes out clean. A warning however – done too early, this test can deflate a cake.

Cooling

Even when cakes or tarts are cooled in the tin, they should still be cooled on a wire rack to avoid the bottom becoming soggy.

Coulis

A sauce of fresh fruit puree, sieved and sweetened. For about one litre of raspberry or blackcurrant coulis, combine one kilo of fruit and 500 to 600 grams of sugar. Heat just enough to dissolve the sugar, but not enough to cook the fruit. Mash the fruit manually or in a food processor and sieve. Some fruits may be helped by a little lemon juice.

Egg whites

To help egg whites 'hold up' and so better lighten cakes and mousse mixtures, hold back a tablespoon of the recipe's sugar to add it to the egg whites as you finish beating them. Also lighten the cake mixture with a generous spoonful of egg white, stirred in, to allow you to fold in the rest of them.

Measurements

Chefs use careful measurements in dessert and cake-making. At home, great cakes have been made by pure guesswork. We all have different priorities. I would value a set of scales above a microwave, for example.

Precision is not so important in savoury dishes such as casseroles but very important in desserts and cakes where a 'chemical' balance of ingredients will ensure that they succeed. An egg short and your cake may be heavy; a longer stick of celery and no one will know.

Method

Throughout, I have assumed the use of a food processor. When cooking, if you haven't used your food processor, you've worked too hard. Using a machine today ensures that you still have time to enjoy cooking, rather than not cook at all. Naturally, if you prefer, all recipes can be made by hand.

Nuts

Nuts used in cooking have better flavour if they are roasted. Place nuts on a tray in a moderate oven, watch them carefully until they are browned. The aroma that fills the kitchen should tell you that they are ready. Some nuts, such as hazelnuts, should be rubbed to remove the papery skin that can then be blown away. Walnuts seem to have enough flavour naturally.

Pastry

I am realistic enough to know that unless it's made in a food processor, few people today will make pastry. Pastry in a food processor is ridiculously easy. Chop the cold butter into pieces and place in the processor bowl with the other dry ingredients. Process with the on/off or pulse button until they have combined in small crumbs. Add just enough cold water (sometimes an egg is included in the binding ingredients) to form a dough, not too hard, not too wet. Wrap in plastic and allow to rest in a cool place for at least half an hour. Don't put the dough in the refrigerator unless it is a very hot day or it will be too firm to roll out. Resting will make the dough nicely 'plastic' and easy to roll out without breaking. Left-over cuttings of pastry are usually over-worked and will not roll out a second time. They can be stored in the freezer. This special rest will make them 'plastic' again for next time.

Soft Centres

These desserts are neither cakes nor creams. They are 'soft' desserts that exploit chocolate's creaminess.

CHOCOLATE GANACHE CAKE

To serve 12 to 16

This is the ultimate celebration cake and it can be made to look spectacular. The use of good ingredients is essential – it is, quite simply, an enormous chocolate truffle! I make it in a French collapsible log tin, approximately 40 cm long. It can in fact be made up into any shape you have.

For the cake . . .

180 g butter
110 g caster sugar
4 eggs, separated
85 g dark chocolate, melted
60 g plain flour

- Hold back one tablespoon of sugar.
- Cream together the butter and remaining sugar until pale and creamy.
- Stir in the egg yolks, then the chocolate.
- Whip the egg whites, adding the last tablespoon of sugar near the end.
- Stir a generous spoonful of the egg whites into the mixture to lighten it, then gently fold in the rest.
- Spread the mixture into a well-buttered and floured Swiss Roll tin, approx 32 cm by 40 cm, and bake in a moderate oven (180°C) for about 10 to 15 minutes.
- Turn out onto a rack to cool.

To make the Ganache . . .

350 ml cream
285 g dark chocolate
4 tbsp overproof kirsch (or other liqueur)

- Over gentle heat, melt the chocolate in the cream, stirring until the mixture is smooth.
- Add the kirsch.
- Allow to cool completely.

To finish the Chocolate Ganache Cake . . .

- With a long ruler, cut the cake lengthwise into 4 strips to line the base and two sides of a 40 cm log tin (the remaining strip will be used for the top of the cake).
- If the tin is not collapsible, make strong 'handles' of greaseproof paper and place under and up the side of the cake to help remove it later.
- When cold, beat the Ganache until it becomes thick and pale.
- Spread it into the cake-lined tin.
- Smooth the top before pressing on the cake 'lid'.
- Allow to chill in the refrigerator for at least 6 hours.
- To serve, unmould onto a long serving platter and dust with cocoa and icing sugar.
- Serve in thin slices with cream and a red berry coulis.

This dessert can also be made up in a square tin, using the cake for a top and bottom only.

CHOCOLATE MOUSSE

The easiest and best Chocolate Mousse as devised by Elizabeth David had a charmingly simple formula. 'For each person allow 1 ounce of chocolate and 1 egg.' In metric the recipe now reads:

For each person, allow 30 g dark chocolate to 1 egg

- Separate the eggs.
- Over a double boiler, melt the chocolate.
- Beat the egg yolks into the chocolate.
- Whip the egg whites and fold gently into the chocolate mixture.
- Flavour with a teaspoon of alcohol per person or the grated rind of an orange for every 4 people.
- Pour into small individual cups or tiny soufflé dishes.
- Chill to set before serving.

WARM CHOCOLATE FONDANT

To serve 6

A delicate warm chocolate pudding from chef Marc Vaca at Chloé's Restaurant in Adelaide.

110 g butter
90 g icing sugar
45 g plain flour
40 g almond meal
90 g dark chocolate, warm and melted
1 tbsp honey
3 egg whites, stiffly beaten

- In a small saucepan, heat the butter until it turns brown (noisette butter). Strain it and set aside.
- In a bowl, mix together the icing sugar, flour and almond meal.
- Stir in the melted chocolate and the still-warm noisette butter.
- Straight away add the honey.
- When the mixture has cooled a little, carefully mix in the beaten egg whites.
- Cook the fondants in 12 small well-buttered and floured moulds, in a low to moderate oven (175°C) for 12 minutes.
- Serve turned out onto plates with vanilla ice-cream and a red fruit coulis.

BITTERSWEET CHOCOLATE SOUFFLÉS

To serve 6

Damien Pignolet's soufflés served at Bistro Moncur in the Woollahra Hotel, Sydney, should dispel the myth that soufflés are temperamental desserts. These are reheated when ready to serve, and can be made up to three days in advance.

For the soufflés

60 g cocoa
85 g caster sugar
180 ml milk
15 g custard powder
30 ml cognac or brandy
3 egg yolks
5 egg whites
100 g dark chocolate, chopped
Soft butter, a little flour and sugar to coat the moulds

- Dissolve cocoa and 60 g of the caster sugar in the milk over a medium heat and bring to the boil.
- Mix the custard powder with some cold water and, off the heat, mix into the milk mixture.
- Return the milk mixture to the boil and beat with a whisk for three minutes to cook out the custard starch.
- Off the heat, beat in the cognac or brandy and allow to cool a little.
- When the custard is warm, not hot, turn it into a bowl and beat in the egg yolks.
- Beat the egg whites stiffly, adding the rest of the caster sugar (25 g) for a satin-like meringue.
- Fold a quarter of the meringue into the custard mix to lighten it.
- Scatter the chocolate over the remaining meringue, add the lightened custard and fold in lightly and quickly.

- Butter 6 moulds (about 240 ml capacity, either metal moulds or ceramic soufflé dishes) and dust with a mixture of flour and sugar.
- Bake at 180°C in a baking dish half-filled with hot water for 12 minutes. The soufflés should be springy to the touch.
- Remove from the oven and allow to cool in the dish of water. Store in the refrigerator until ready to use.

To serve

10 g instant coffee
1 tbsp cognac or brandy
600 ml cream
1 tsp vanilla essence
icing sugar

- Dissolve the coffee in the tablespoon of cognac or brandy.
- Bring the cream to the boil and carefully reduce it to about 400 ml.
- Add the coffee mixture and vanilla and simmer for another minute.
- Unmould the soufflés by dipping the moulds in hot water for a moment.
- Arrange them on an oven-proof serving dish and pour the cream over and around them.
- Bake at 180°C for about 8 minutes until well-risen.

Alternatively, you may wish to serve the soufflés individually as in restaurant service, where, when ordered, a soufflé is placed on an individual gratin dish for reheating in the oven.

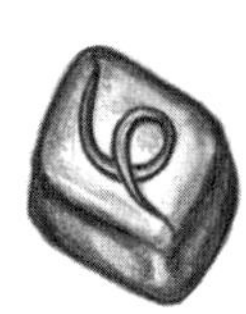

CHOCOLATE RISOTTO (CHOCOLATE RICE PUDDING)

To serve 4 as a family, 6 at a dinner party

1 tbsp butter
1 cup arborio rice
2 cups water
½ tsp salt
1 cup milk
1 cup cream
150 g dark chocolate, chopped into small pieces
2 tbsp sugar (or dark brown sugar)
2 tsp good vanilla extract or ½ tsp pure orange oil

- Melt the butter in a saucepan and add the rice.
- Cook the rice, stirring occasionally, for about 5 minutes or until it becomes opaque.
- Add the water and salt.
- Bring to the boil, turn down the heat right down, cover and simmer until the water is absorbed and the surface of the rice is covered in small holes.
- Turn up the heat slightly, stir in the milk and cook until the milk has been absorbed.
- Add the cream and continue to cook on low heat for a further 5 minutes.
- Add the chocolate and stir until melted.
- Finish with the sugar and vanilla or orange oil.
- Turn off the heat. Cover the rice and allow it to sit for 10 minutes before serving warm.
- For a family dish, serve with sliced banana and vanilla ice-cream. To end a grand dinner, serve small portions with cream and walnut ice-cream.

Dessert Cakes

Technically these are cakes, but they are special enough to finish a great meal and delicate enough to require cutlery!

CHOCOLATE DIVA CAKE WITH CUMQUAT SAUCE

To serve 12

Kelly Sugar Leonard is dessert chef at Janet Jeffs' Juniperberry restaurant in Canberra. The initial work of beating the mixture may seem tedious but the cake is easy after that and has a sublime texture. The different alcohols can be modified to suit what you have in the cupboard.

For the cake . . .

9 eggs
120 g raw sugar
500 g dark chocolate, melted
200 g single cream, whipped
½ tsp ground cinnamon
3 tbsp kirsch
3 tbsp Grand Marnier
2 tbsp rum

- Prepare a 30 cm, preferably teflon-coated tin by lining the bottom with greaseproof paper.
- Place the eggs and sugar in a stainless steel bowl over a saucepan of simmering water on the stove.
- With an electric beater (or by hand if you're strong!) beat the mixture for about 10 minutes until it is thick and creamy in colour.
- Off the heat carefully fold in the chocolate, then the cream and finally the cinnamon and alcohols.
- Pour the mixture into the tin and place it in a baking dish filled with hot water.
- Cook in a moderate oven (180°C) for 60 to 75 minutes.

- Remove from the oven and allow it to cool in the tin on a wire rack.
- Turn out and dust with icing sugar.
- The cake can be refrigerated and will be easier to cut, although the texture may not be as delicate.

For the sauce . . .

500 g cumquats, halved and seeded.
500 g caster sugar
1 cinnamon stick
3 cardamon pods
1 litre water

- Combine all ingredients in a saucepan, with enough water to cover the fruit.
- Bring to the boil and simmer for 1 hour, adding more water if necessary.
- Set aside and cool.
- Remove cinnamon stick and cardamon pods, and serve sauce spooned over the cake.

CHOCOLATE AND DATE MERINGUE CAKE

To serve 8

This recipe comes from Rosa Matto's Cookery School in Adelaide. Its combination of cake ingredients is delicious but also try changing to walnuts or pecans, roasted hazelnuts, chopped Australian apricots or nectarines and so on. Make the cake the day before it is to be served.

6 egg whites
110 g caster sugar
200 g unblanched almonds, roasted and chopped
250 g dark chocolate, chopped into small pieces
250 g pitted dates, finely chopped
whipped cream

- Beat egg whites until stiff, gradually adding caster sugar to make a glossy meringue.
- Fold in almonds, chocolate and dates.
- Spoon into a buttered, foil-lined 23 cm springform pan.
- Bake in a low to moderate oven (160°C) for 1 hour. Allow to cool in the oven.
- Gently remove from the cake tin, place on a plate, cover and chill overnight.
- Do not use on the day it is made, it is too crumbly.
- Cover with whipped cream. This is good to eat and will also hide the fact that the fragile cake might be misshapen!
- Decorate with toasted flaked almonds or chopped chocolate as you wish.

QUEEN OF SHEBA

To serve 8 to 10

The taste of this completely flourless dessert relies on the quality of the chocolate; the secret of its texture relies on the cooking. There is a temptation to over-cook it, that is cook it until the whole cake is firm. The centre must remain soft. When cool, the cake will set and have a fudge-like consistency.

250 g dark chocolate.
225 g butter
90 g caster sugar
5 eggs
2 tbsp rum, brandy or liqueur of your choice
1 tbsp plain flour, sifted

- Hold back a tbsp of sugar.
- Melt and stir together the chocolate, butter and remaining sugar in a small saucepan over low heat.
- Allow to cool a little, while, in a bowl, you beat the eggs and the reserved sugar until pale.
- Stir in the chocolate mixture, alcohol and finally the sifted flour.
- Pour into a well-buttered and floured 23 cm solid cake tin, its bottom lined with a circle of greaseproof paper.
- Place the tin in a baking dish filled with hot water and bake in a moderate oven (180°C) for about 30 minutes until the edge is cooked and the centre still soft. It will take courage to trust that it is cooked enough.
- Allow cake to cool in the tin on a cooling rack. It may sink slightly in the centre.
- To serve, run a knife around the edge and turn onto a plate. Carefully peel back the greaseproof paper and discard.
- Dust lightly with icing sugar and serve with whipped cream or a coulis of berry fruits.

The Mistress's Own

No Australian chocolate book could ignore Ann Oliver's contribution to chocolate desserts. A meticulous chef, she created 'The Chocolate Slut' at her old restaurant, Mistress Augustine's in Adelaide, especially for a client (male incidentally) who was besotted by chocolate. The clever recipe below leads on to make two other desserts. Egg size is important in these recipes. You will need 10 soufflé moulds of 200 ml each.

THE MISTRESS'S OWN CHOCOLATE SOUFFLÉ

To serve 10

12 extra large eggs (61 g) or 14 large (55 g)
500 g butter, very soft
Butter for buttering the soufflé moulds
350 g caster sugar
300 g dark chocolate, melted
Cocoa for dusting

- Place the eggs in a bowl of hot water to warm them.
- Whisk the butter until pale. Add half the caster sugar and continue beating until the mixture is creamy.
- Separate the eggs and add the yolks one at a time to the butter mixture.
- Add the warm, melted chocolate and whisk through the butter mixture.
- Beat the egg whites until they form soft peaks, adding the remaining caster sugar near the end.
- Carefully fold the egg whites into the chocolate mixture until completely incorporated. The mixture should be smooth and glossy.
- Butter the soufflé moulds, taking care to reach the inner ridge and rim of each mould.
- Divide the mixture evenly into the moulds.

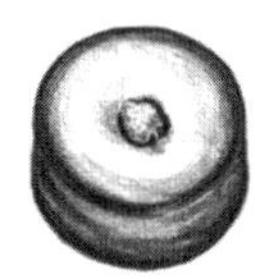

- Arrange the moulds on two baking sheets and cook for about 20 minutes in a pre-heated oven of 175°C until the soufflés rise to double their original size.
- Dust with cocoa and serve immediately with vanilla or mocha ice-cream or pouring cream.

LA STUPENDA CHOCOLATE TORTE

To serve 8 to 10

1 x 12 egg quantity The Mistress's Own Chocolate Soufflé mixture
150 g dark chocolate, finely chipped
150 ml butter, melted and clarified
3 extra large egg yolks
2 tbsp Grand Marnier
Additional chocolate for decorating the dessert or chocolate sprinkles

- Prepare the Mistress's Own Chocolate Soufflé mixture as in the previous recipe (up to the sixth step).
- Butter a 25 cm seamless cake tin. Line the base with paper and the sides to at least 4 cm above the rim of the tin.
- Pour the freshly made soufflé mixture into the prepared tin. Place it in a baking dish of hot water in a pre-heated oven of 150°C for 90 minutes, taking care that the top does not burn.
- Out of the oven, run a knife carefully around the edge of the tin and stand on a rack to cool.
- When cold, run a knife around the edge once more and invert onto a tray.
- Melt the chocolate and clarified butter together, either in the microwave or over a double boiler. Stir well and allow to cool a little.

- Whisk the egg yolks and Grand Marnier together in a bowl. Whisking constantly, work in the chocolate mixture, whisking it until it is thick and glossy. If the chocolate mixture is too hot the glaze will not work.
- Spread the glaze over the top of the torte and allow to set.
- Decorate the torte lavishly with tempered chocolate curls made from the additional chocolate or simply with a scattering of chocolate sprinkles.
- The torte must not be refrigerated, but left in a cool place. It will keep several days in perfect condition.

FIG AND CHOCOLATE MOUSSE GATEAU

To serve 12 or more

Half quantity of The Mistress's Own Chocolate Soufflé mixture
1 tsp sweet oil – apricot or almond
420 g dark chocolate, finely chopped
150 ml butter, clarified
4 extra large eggs, separated
130 g caster sugar
1 tbsp cognac
800 ml thickened cream, whipped to soft peaks
16 large ripe figs, peeled and cut in half lengthwise

- Butter a 28 cm spring form tin and line the base with paper.
- As it may leak a little, place the tin on a baking tray. Pour in the Mistress's Own Chocolate Soufflé and bake for 35 to 45 minutes at 175°C.
- Allow to cool on a rack before removing the ring and very carefully inverting the cake, with its base still attached, onto a serving plate.
- Carefully remove the base and paper.

- Wash the ring, brush it with sweet oil and place it back around the cake, pushing the edge of the cake against the edge of the tin if it is smaller than the tin.
- Refrigerate while making the mousse as follows.

For the mousse . . .

- Place the chocolate and butter in a double boiler and stir until just melted.
- In another bowl, whisk the egg yolks with the sugar and cognac until the sugar has dissolved.
- When the chocolate mixture has cooled a little, stir the egg yolks into the mixture.
- Carefully fold in the cream.
- Whisk the egg whites to soft peaks and fold into the mixture.
- Cut 8 figs in half lengthwise and press the cut edge up against the cake tin on top of the cake to form a border.
- Pour three-quarters of the mousse mixture into the cake tin, jiggling it very carefully to smooth the top. Put the remaining mousse into a piping bag.
- Cover the gateau with plastic and refrigerate for at least six hours, preferably overnight.
- Put the piping bag into a closed container in the refrigerator.

To finish . . .

- To finish the cake, allow the piping bag mousse to soften a little out of refrigerator before piping 16 rosettes around the edge of the cake.
- Cut the remaining figs in half lengthwise and place, cut side up, on each rosette.
- Carefully run a knife around the edge of the cake and remove the ring before serving.

Pots of Chocolate

Chocolate creams, too delicate to stand on their own.

MOCHA CUSTARD

To serve 8

Chocolate makes a custard even silkier. This delicate combination of chocolate and coffee comes from Stephanie Alexander, restaurateur and writer.

1 tsp instant coffee
30 g freshly ground coffee beans
500 ml milk
1 vanilla pod, split in two
100 g dark chocolate
100 g caster sugar
½ cup cold water
3 tbsp boiling water
6 egg yolks
2 whole eggs

- Put instant coffee, ground coffee, milk and vanilla pod in a saucepan and bring slowly to simmering point, stirring frequently.
- Simmer for 30 minutes, very gently.
- Strain through a double piece of muslin to extract all the coffee grains.
- Return the milk mixture to a clean pan with the chocolate and heat until the chocolate is completely melted and quite smooth.
- Strain again through a fine strainer.
- Dissolve the sugar in the cold water and cook until it is a deep, golden caramel.

- Taking care to stand well back, pour the 3 tbsp of boiling water onto the caramel and allow to dissolve into a smooth caramel syrup.
- Pour the syrup into the chocolate and milk mixture and stir. Set aside until cool.
- Whisk the egg yolks and eggs and pour on the chocolate mixture. Strain again.
- Pour the mixture into individual porcelain mousse pots and place them on a wet folded cloth in the bottom of a baking dish.
- Fill the dish up to half-way with boiling water, cover with foil and bake at 150°C for 1 to 1¼ hours or until just set.
- The custard will firm up when cold but is not meant to be unmoulded.

MOCHA AND AMARETTI CUSTARD

To make 12 small servings

Michael Voumard of the Botanic Dining Room in Adelaide procures cocoa liquor for this chocolate 'trifle'. You can replace it with an extra 50 grams of dark chocolate and 1 tbsp cocoa.

600 ml milk
400 ml cream
5 tbsp ground coffee beans
12 egg yolks
350 g caster sugar
270 g dark chocolate
70 g cocoa liquor
36 amaretti biscuits

- Place the milk, cream and ground coffee in a saucepan and bring to the boil.
- Meanwhile whisk the egg yolks and sugar together until creamy.
- Strain the milk onto the yolk and sugar mixture and return to the saucepan.
- Stir continuously over low heat until slightly thickened. Do not let it boil.
- Strain the custard mixture into a bowl and allow to cool.
- Melt the chocolate and cocoa liquor (or chocolate with cocoa) in a bowl over a saucepan of hot water.
- When both the chocolate and custard are at blood temperature, gradually whisk the custard into the chocolate.
- Place three amaretti biscuits into each of 12 small serving dishes.
- Pour the chocolate mixture over the amaretti and refrigerate for at least four hours.
- Serve if you wish with almond biscotti.

DARK AND MILK CHOCOLATE POTS

To make 12 small pots

The beauty of this simple recipe is the serving of two small pots to each person for a contrast of flavours. One pot could also be made with white chocolate. The recipe comes from Sue-Ellen Hope and Pierre Barelier of The Wild Olive Restaurant, Nuriootpa, in South Australia's Barossa Valley.

75 g dark chocolate, chopped
75 g milk (or white) chocolate, chopped
8 egg yolks
145 g caster sugar
500 ml milk
5 extra tbsp milk

- Bring the 500 ml milk to the boil and pour half into one bowl, half into another.
- Off the heat, add the dark chocolate to one bowl and the milk chocolate to the other. Stir until melted.
- Whisk egg yolks and caster sugar together until creamy.
- Add half the mixture to each of the bowls.
- Pour the dark chocolate mixture into 6 small porcelain pots, and the milk chocolate mixture into another 6 pots.
- Place pots in a baking dish filled with hot water and cook at 160°C for about 30 minutes or until the mixture is set.
- Serve chilled.
- The mixtures can also be cooked in two ceramic soufflé dishes.

Tarts

The perfect combination of crisp pastry and a tender centre.

CHOCOLATE TRUFFLE TART

To serve 8 to 10

Pastry made with 200 g butter, 400 g flour, ½ cup cold water, 1½ tbsp cocoa, 1 tbsp caster sugar
400 g dark chocolate
300 ml single cream
100 ml milk
2 eggs

- Make the pastry and allow it to rest for at least ½ hour before rolling it out thinly.
- Line a 24 cm loose-bottomed tin with the pastry. Prick the base with a fork and chill in the fridge or freezer for 15 minutes.
- Bake blind in a moderate oven (180°C) for 15 minutes
- Meanwhile, heat the cream and milk.
- Add the chopped chocolate and stir until dissolved.
- Off the heat, beat the mixture until it is smooth and shiny. Stir in the eggs.
- Pour the chocolate mixture into the tin and bake in a low to moderate oven (160°C) for about 15 to 20 minutes until firm but not hard.
- Allow to cool a while on a rack before sliding off the tin and base.
- Serve just warm.

BAKED CHOCOLATE TART WITH ESPRESSO ICE-CREAM

To serve 10 to 12

Philip Johnson's dessert from e'cco bistro, Brisbane, exploits the symbiosis of chocolate and coffee. You will need an ice-cream machine.

For the ice-cream

300 g caster sugar
12 egg yolks
500 ml milk
500 ml cream
120 g ground coffee beans

- Lightly whisk the caster sugar and egg yolks.
- Combine milk, cream and ground coffee in a saucepan and heat until almost boiling.
- Whisk hot milk mixture into egg mixture and return to saucepan over medium heat.
- Stir well until custard thickens, taking care not to boil.
- Pass through a fine sieve and refrigerate until cold.
- Churn ice-cream and keep in the freezer until needed.

For the tart base

350 g butter
150 g icing sugar
4 egg yolks
50 ml water
500 g flour

- Cream together butter and icing sugar in a food processor, then add egg yolks, one at a time, then water.
- Remove mixture from the machine and fold in the flour.

- Wrap in plastic and chill for 2 hours.
- Roll out pastry to 5 mm thick.
- Line a 24 cm loose-bottomed tart tin with the pastry and chill in the refrigerator for one hour.
- Bake blind at 200°C for 10 minutes.
- Remove from oven, remove weights and lining, and return tart case to the oven until golden.
- This can be done 24 hours before use.

For the filling

375 g dark chocolate
250 g butter
2 eggs
5 egg yolks
75 g caster sugar
cocoa for dusting the finished tart

- Melt together the chocolate and butter.
- Whisk eggs, egg yolks and sugar until creamy.
- Mix together the chocolate and egg mixtures and pour into cooked tart shell.
- Bake tart for about 10 minutes at 130°C. Custard should be beginning to set around the edges but still wobbly in the centre.
- Dust tart with cocoa to serve. Serve it at room temperature, with the espresso ice-cream.

CHOCOLATE FIG AND NUT TART

To serve 8 to 10

This recipe comes from Justin Harmon at The Salopian Inn, McLaren Vale, South Australia.

Pastry made with 175 g flour, 110 g butter, 1 tsp sugar, 1 small egg yolk, 1 tbsp milk
75 g dried figs, chopped
250 g dark chocolate, chopped
1½ tbsp brandy
110 ml cream
30 g butter
3 tbsp caster sugar
1½ tbsp honey
¼ tsp ground aniseed (optional)
60 g pine nuts
30 g slivered almonds
90 g whole almonds, roughly chopped

- Make the pastry and allow to rest for 30 minutes.
- The pastry will be soft and needs to be rolled out between sheets of baking paper.
- Line a 23 cm loose-bottomed tart tin with the pastry. Alternatively, simply press the pastry into the tin.
- Chill for 30 minutes then line with aluminium foil and beans to bake blind at 200°C for 5 minutes.
- Meanwhile place all remaining ingredients in a saucepan and cook over gentle heat, stirring, until chocolate has melted and mixture is smooth.
- Pour into pastry case and bake in a moderate oven (180°C) for 15 to 20 minutes.
- Cool before serving.

Chocolate Cakes and Biscuits

These recipes could fill up a lunch-box or a picnic basket. Don't assume, however, that they can not stand up to more elegant situations.

BROWNIES

Possibly America's greatest contribution to baking, the brownie is the perfect blend of chocolate and nut. The mixture, not quite cake, not quite biscuit, should be slightly chewy, with the eggs and chocolate just holding the other ingredients in place with the help of as little flour as possible. Walnuts are a standard with brownies but any nut marries well with chocolate. If using hazelnuts, make sure to roast them first for better flavour and then rub and blow off the skins.

275 g butter 10 oz
500 g dark chocolate 1 lb. +
5 eggs
410 g caster sugar 14 oz +
135 g plain flour 5 oz
500 g walnuts or other nuts 1 lb
200 g sultanas (optional) 8 oz

- Melt together the butter and chocolate.
- Beat the eggs and caster sugar together until pale and creamy.
- Stir the chocolate mixture into the egg and sugar.
- Sift the flour over the mixture and fold in.
- Add the nuts and sultanas and fold in.
- Pour into a well-buttered and floured tin, about 24 cm by 30 cm.
- Bake in a moderate oven (180°C) for 40 minutes.

- The brownies should be cooked but still a little soft in the centre.
- Allow to cool in the tin, sitting on a cooling rack.
- Turn out onto a board and cut into squares or fingers, dusted with icing sugar if you like.

SPICED CHOCOLATE TEA BISCUITS

To make 35 to 40 biscuits

110 g caster sugar
200 g butter
70 g dark chocolate, melted
300 g plain flour
5 tbsp cornflour
1 tbsp cocoa
¼ tsp each of ground cinnamon, coriander and cardamon

- Beat together the sugar and butter until pale and creamy.
- Add the melted chocolate.
- Mix together the flours, cocoa and spices. Add to the mixture and work to a crumbly dough.
- On a sheet of aluminium foil, form the dough into a log and roll it in the foil.
- Chill until firm or freeze until needed.
- Remove the foil, cut log into ½ cm slices and place them on a baking sheet.
- Bake in a low to moderate oven (175°C) for about 15 minutes.
- Remove biscuits from the oven and cool on a wire rack.

WALNUT AND CITRUS CAKE

This cake, with its concentrated flavours of chocolate, citrus and walnuts, can be cut into small fingers and served as a confectionery with coffee.

175 g walnuts
150 g caster sugar
5 eggs, separated
150 g dark chocolate, coarsely grated
Grated rind of 1 orange or 1 lemon
60 g mixed candied citrus peel, finely chopped

- Butter a shallow tin about 24 cm by 30 cm and dust with a mixture of plain flour and breadcrumbs, or line the bottom of the tin with greaseproof paper.
- In a food processor, grind the walnuts to resemble coarse breadcrumbs.
- Hold back a tbsp of caster sugar.
- Beat together the egg yolks and remaining sugar until thick and creamy.
- Fold in the walnuts, orange or lemon rind and candied peel.
- Whip the egg whites until stiff, adding the reserved sugar near the end.
- To lighten the walnut chocolate mixture, stir in 1 large spoon of egg whites, then gently fold in the rest.
- Bake in a moderate oven (180°C) for ¾ to 1 hour, until cake is cooked.
- Remove from oven. When it has cooled a little, turn out onto a cooling rack.
- Cut into squares or fingers and dust with icing sugar to serve.

DAY AND NIGHT CAKE

To serve 8

6 eggs, separated
190 g caster sugar
70 g dark chocolate, melted
145 g walnuts, ground to fine crumbs
145 g ground blanched almonds
½ tsp almond essence (optional)
1 tsp lemon juice or white wine vinegar (to keep the meringue soft)

- Beat the egg yolks and half the caster sugar until pale and creamy.
- Stir in the chocolate, then the walnuts.
- Spread mixture into a 20–22 cm spring-form cake tin, the base lined with greaseproof paper.
- Whip the egg whites until soft peaks form. Gradually add the remaining caster sugar to form a stiff meringue.
- Fold the ground almonds, almond essence and lemon juice or vinegar into the meringue mixture.
- Spread this over the chocolate walnut mixture.
- Bake in a low to moderate oven (170°C) for 1 hour or until the meringue is cooked.
- Allow to cool in the tin a little on a cooling rack before releasing the sides and sliding the cake off the base.
- The cake is rich enough to be simply dusted with icing sugar. Otherwise, when cold, spread with 80 g of chocolate melted with 1 tbsp butter.

CHOCOLATE CAKE ICED WITH CHOCOLATE FROSTING

As chocolate contains a fat (cocoa butter), cake-making with good quality cocoa achieves lightness without a mountain of egg whites. This is a simply perfect cake with good flavour and delicate texture.

For the cake . . .

185 g butter
1½ cups caster sugar
½ cup cocoa
½ cup hot water
3 eggs
¼ tsp bicarbonate of soda
2 cups self-raising flour
¾ cup milk
2 tsp real vanilla essence

- Cream together butter and caster sugar.
- Mix together the cocoa and water and stir into the butter mixture.
- One by one, beat in the eggs.
- Sift together the bicarbonate of soda and the flour.
- Stir into the chocolate mixture, alternating with milk and vanilla.
- Pour into a well-buttered and floured 24 cm springform cake tin, base lined with greaseproof paper.
- Bake in a moderate oven (180°C) for about an hour.

For the Chocolate Frosting . . .

100 g butter
150 g dark chocolate

- Melt together the chocolate and butter.
- Allow to cool a little before beating well.
- When slightly thickened, spread over cake.

DEVIL'S FOOD CAKE

To serve 8

So named because it is the deepest, darkest chocolate cake.

175 g dark chocolate, chopped
250 ml milk
225 g caster sugar
2 eggs, separated
125 g butter
250 g plain flour
2 tbsp cocoa
2½ tsp baking powder
1 tsp good vanilla essence

- Over low heat, melt the chocolate in one-third of the milk.
- Dissolve in half the sugar and, off the heat, stir in the egg yolks until smooth.
- Beat together the butter and the rest of the sugar until pale and creamy.
- Sift together the flour, cocoa and baking powder.
- Fold the flour mixture into the creamed butter mixture, along with the rest of the milk and the vanilla essence.
- Stir in the chocolate mixture.
- Beat the egg whites until stiff and fold into the cake batter.
- Pour into a well-buttered and floured 20 cm cake tin, the base lined with greaseproof paper.
- Bake in a moderate oven (180°C) for about 45 minutes.
- Cool a little in the tin before turning out onto a cooling rack.
- Cover the top and sides with chocolate icing.

CHOCOLATE AND ALMOND CAKE

To serve 6 to 8

Chocolate and almonds are often seen together in cakes. Not only do they work well together as flavours but using almond meal with chocolate makes the cake lighter and less dense. The recipe below makes a simple but nonetheless delicate cake. To make a larger quantity, double the mixture but bake in two small tins.

150 g dark chocolate
90 g butter
75 g caster sugar
4 eggs, separated
90 g ground almonds

- Melt the chocolate and butter together.
- Hold back 1 tbsp of sugar. Beat together the remaining sugar and the egg yolks until thick and creamy.
- Stir in the chocolate mixture, then the almonds.
- Pour into a well-buttered and floured cake tin (20 cm) its base lined with greaseproof paper.
- Bake in a low to moderate oven (175°C) for about 45 minutes.
- Use as a cake lightly dusted with icing sugar and cocoa or as a dessert served with cream and possibly red berries.

CHOCOLATE ICING

40 g dark chocolate
180 g icing sugar
40 g butter
2 tbsp milk
2 tsp honey

- Place all ingredients into a saucepan and combine together over gentle heat.
- Remove the saucepan from the heat.
- Stir mixture vigorously as it cools until it thickens enough to spread.

CHOCOLATE WHISKY CAKE WITH PRUNES

This recipe comes from Maggie Beer, restaurateur and writer. It is best made the day before serving and kept under plastic wrap.

½ cup prunes, pitted and cut into small pieces
½ cup whisky
420 g dark chocolate
6 tbsp water
250 g butter, cut into small pieces
6 eggs, separated
300 g caster sugar
300 g roasted almonds, finely ground
9 tbsp plain flour, sifted
Pinch of cream of tartar

- Allow the prunes to soak in the whisky overnight.
- Melt chocolate with water in a double boiler.
- Off the heat, stir in the butter.

- Beat together the egg yolks and caster sugar in a bowl until thick and creamy.
- Stir in the chocolate and butter mixture.
- Fold in the ground almonds, sifted flour, prunes and whisky.
- Beat the egg whites with the cream of tartar until stiff.
- Stir a generous spoonful of egg whites into the mixture to lighten it before gently folding in the rest.
- Pour into a buttered and floured 23 cm spring-form tin, the base lined with greaseproof paper.
- Bake in a moderate oven (190°C) for 20 to 30 minutes until just firm to the touch. Do not over-cook.
- Allow the cake to cool a little in the tin before removing it.
- To serve, dust with icing sugar.

AVIGNON CHOCOLATE CAKE

To serve 6 to 8

This recipe was collected by writer Barbara Santich from a small restaurant in France. The cake now appears regularly for Santich family birthdays. While it can be eaten the day that it is made, it is usually better the next day when the chocolate cream and cake have had time to come together. Store it in a cool place.

2 eggs
150 g caster sugar
60 g icing sugar
2 tbsp ground almonds
3 additional egg whites
2½ tbsp good quality cocoa
65 g plain flour
150 g dark chocolate, chopped
300 ml cream

- Lightly beat eggs with sugar, then mix in icing sugar and ground almonds.
- Beat egg whites until stiff and fold into the mixture.
- Sift together cocoa and flour and fold in lightly.
- Pour mixture into a well-buttered and floured spring-form cake tin (20 cm or 23 cm), base lined with greaseproof paper.
- Smooth the surface and bake in a low oven (120°C) for about an hour for 20 cm tin or 45 minutes for 23 cm tin.
- Cool slightly in the tin before unmoulding.
- For the ganache icing, gently melt the chocolate in the cream over low heat.
- Allow to cool slightly then whisk until thick and a pale creamy chocolate colour.
- Spread over top and sides of cake.

Frozen Desserts

I am sure you know about the allure of chocolate in ice-cream, parfaits, sorbets . . .

TERRINE OF THREE CHOCOLATE ICE-CREAMS ON A MOCHA ANGLAISE WITH HAZELNUT PRALINE

To serve 8

Mietta's Queenscliff Hotel in Victoria makes a 36-egg-yolk quantity of this recipe. As it is time-consuming but worth the effort, you might consider making a double quantity yourself. You will need an ice-cream maker.

1 vanilla pod
750 ml hot milk
9 egg yolks
100 g caster sugar
175 g dark chocolate
2 tbsp coarsely ground coffee beans
175 g white chocolate
185 g milk chocolate
260 ml thickened cream

- Split vanilla pod lengthways, add to milk and bring to boil.
- Lightly beat egg yolks with caster sugar.
- Pour hot milk over yolks and sugar, stirring constantly.
- Return to very low heat and stir with a spatula until thickened just enough to coat the back of a spoon. Take care not to over-cook or over-heat.
- Remove from heat.
- Divide the mixture (the crème anglaise) into four bowls.
- To the first bowl, add and stir in the ground coffee and 25 g of the dark chocolate. This makes the mocha anglaise, which will be used as the sauce. Set aside.

- To the next bowl, add the white chocolate and stir until dissolved.
- To the third bowl, add the milk chocolate, and to the fourth add the remaining 150 g dark chocolate. Stir until dissolved.
- Allow to cool, then add one-third of the cream to each of the last three bowls.
- Churn one bowl of ice cream at a time and layer in a terrine mould, starting with the white chocolate, then milk, then dark. Freeze overnight.

For the praline . . .

50 g caster sugar
25 ml water
50 g roasted hazelnuts, peeled

- Dissolve sugar and water in a saucepan over low heat.
- Turn the heat up and allow to cook till caramelised.
- Add the hazelnuts.
- Pour onto a buttered plate and allow to set. When cool, crush into small pieces.
- To serve, pour a pool of mocha anglaise into the centre of each plate. Turn out the ice-cream terrine and cut into 2 cm slices. Place a slice onto the mocha anglaise on each plate. Sprinkle praline around the plate.

ICED CHOCOLATE PARFAIT

To serve 8

The trouble with ice-cream recipes is that to have really smooth ice-cream, the mixture needs to be churned and frozen in an ice-cream machine. This mixture, however, is so rich that ice crystals won't form as it freezes and it stays beautifully smooth.

250 ml milk
6 egg yolks
200 g caster sugar
300 g dark chocolate, chopped into small pieces
250 ml cream, whipped

- Heat the milk to just under boiling.
- Beat together the egg yolks and sugar in a bowl until thick and creamy.
- Pour the hot milk over the mixture and stir.
- Pour mixture into a double boiler over simmering water and cook until the mixture thickens and will coat the back of a wooden spoon.
- DO NOT LET IT BOIL – it will curdle.
- Pour the mixture into the bowl of an electric beater.
- On the lowest speed, beat the mixture as you drop the chocolate into it, piece by piece.
- Once all the chocolate has been incorporated and the mixture has cooled, fold in the whipped cream.
- Pour into a log tin and freeze.
- Serve with blackcurrant coulis.

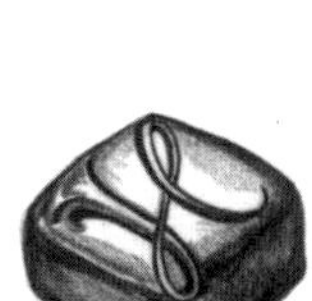

CHAMPAGNE MELON AND WATERMELON GRANITAS WITH CHOCOLATE

This idea comes from Janni Kyritsis of MG Garage Restaurant in Sydney.

Take the flesh of a champagne melon and a watermelon, and pass each one through a fine sieve, separately. Freeze juices in shallow trays, stirring occasionally with a fork to form granita. Once set, scoop a little of each granita into martini glasses and cover with shavings of dark chocolate.

After Dinner

Some chocolate pieces to finish a meal.

BISCOTTI WITH CHOCOLATE AND BLACK PEPPER

To make about 30 biscuits

Blue Wensleydale cheese was once served with chocolate-coated Digestive biscuits. Serve these biscuits with cheese, especially any creamy blue-veined cheese.

2 tbsp cocoa, sifted
2½ cups plain flour with 1 tsp baking powder
¾ cup caster sugar
2 eggs
125 g almonds, toasted in the oven
1 tsp coarsely ground black pepper

- Sift together the cocoa and flour.
- In a food processor, make a firm dough with the flour, caster sugar and eggs. You may need to add a little water but use sparingly.
- Chop the almonds roughly.
- On a floured board, incorporate the almonds and pepper into the dough.

- Divide the dough into three pieces and roll into baguettes.
- Bake in a moderate oven (180°C) for about 20 minutes.
- Cool and then cut into ¾ cm slices.
- Lay slices on a baking tray. Lower the oven to 120°C and cook for a further 20–30 minutes.

CHOCOLATE AND NATIVE PEPPERMINT TOAST

This recipe comes from Andrew Fielke of The Red Ochre Grill restaurants, renowned for using indigenous ingredients. This is classic almond bread with an Australian twist.

170 g flour
10 g cocoa
5 g native peppermint
6 egg whites
180 g sugar
180 g macadamia nuts

- Sift 120 g of the flour into a bowl.
- Into another bowl, sift together remaining 50 g flour, the cocoa and native peppermint.
- Whisk egg whites with a pinch of sugar until soft peaks form. Gradually add the rest of the sugar.
- Remove one-third of the resulting meringue and mix with cocoa mixture.
- Fold in the plain flour and macadamia nuts to remaining meringue mixture.
- Butter and flour a loaf tin. Fill with cocoa meringue, then spoon over the nut meringue.
- Bake in a pre-heated oven at 180°C for 30 minutes.
- Allow to cool, then wrap in plastic and refrigerate overnight.
- Slice thinly and place on baking trays in the oven at 90°C for 20 minutes or until crisp.

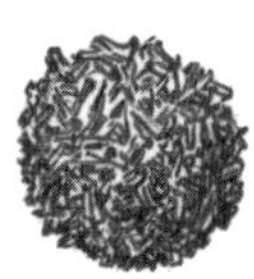

THE RICHEST CUP OF CHOCOLATE

For two people (with a little over)

This is more than a children's cup of cocoa – not that there's anything wrong with cocoa!

The 'thickness' is in the style of European hot chocolate, where you are often served a small jug from which to help yourself. It is also closer than the standard Anglo-Saxon cocoa to the hot chocolate drink of the past.

2 cups of milk (or half milk, half water)
½ tsp ground cinnamon
200 g dark chocolate, broken into pieces
2 tsp of cocoa blended with 2 tsp of cornflour and 2 tbsp of water
1 tbsp of rum, brandy or Cointreau (optional)

- Heat milk and cinnamon in a small saucepan over low heat.
- Stir the chocolate pieces into the milk.
- When the chocolate has completely melted and the mixture is smooth, add the cocoa and cornflour and continue heating just until the chocolate thickens.
- Add the alcohol and serve immediately.

CHOCOLATE SAUCE

To serve 4

This sauce can be served warm or chilled. Serve it over ice-cream or with poached pears for the classic dessert of 'Poires Belle Hélène'.

300 ml cream
250 g dark chocolate
2 tbsp dark brown sugar and 2 tbsp rum; or 1 tbsp dark brown sugar and 2 tbsp Cointreau or other orange liqueur

- Over gentle heat, melt the chocolate into the cream, stirring until the sauce is smooth.
- Add the sugar and alcohol.

CHOCOLATE TRUFFLES

Makes 60 truffles

With so many Haigh's truffles to choose from, there is little point in making chocolates yourself unless you wish to choose a particular flavouring and are committed to using the best ingredients. Paul Merrony provided this recipe for the truffles he serves at Merrony's Restaurant in Sydney and it serves to illustrate the attention to detail required for a good result.

500 ml cream
850 g grated or chopped dark chocolate
50 ml of your preferred spirit (eg Grand Marnier or brandy)
300 g good quality couverture chocolate
300 g cocoa powder

Two days in advance

- Boil cream and pour onto dark chocolate in a bowl.
- Add spirit and mix well with a wooden spoon until chocolate is melted and mixture appears a smooth, shiny, homogeneous mass.
- Scrape down the edges and cover with cling film, pressing down to prevent air from coming into contact with the chocolate.
- Allow this ganache to stand in a cool place.

One day in advance

- Pipe the ganache onto a foil lined tray in 1–1½ cm balls, using a 1 cm plain nozzle. Chill for about 3 hours until set.
- Roll lightly and quickly between your palms to give the truffles a regular, spherical shape. Return them to fridge.

Six hours before serving

- Gently melt couverture chocolate over simmering water. Remove from heat.
- Sift cocoa powder into shallow, plastic container with a lid.
- Using a dipping fork, dip truffles one at a time into melted, blood temperature couverture. After dipping, tap fork to remove excess couverture.
- Place truffles gently onto cocoa powder and repeat dipping/tapping/powdering process until all balls are done.
- The truffles should be arranged neatly and well-separated in the cocoa. Replace lid and return to fridge for two more hours.

Dressing the dish

- Place truffles in a sieve and shake gently to remove excess cocoa powder. This should be done in several batches to avoid cracking the chocolate shell.
- The truffles can stay in the cocoa, covered, for up to a week – if you have the will-power to wait that long.

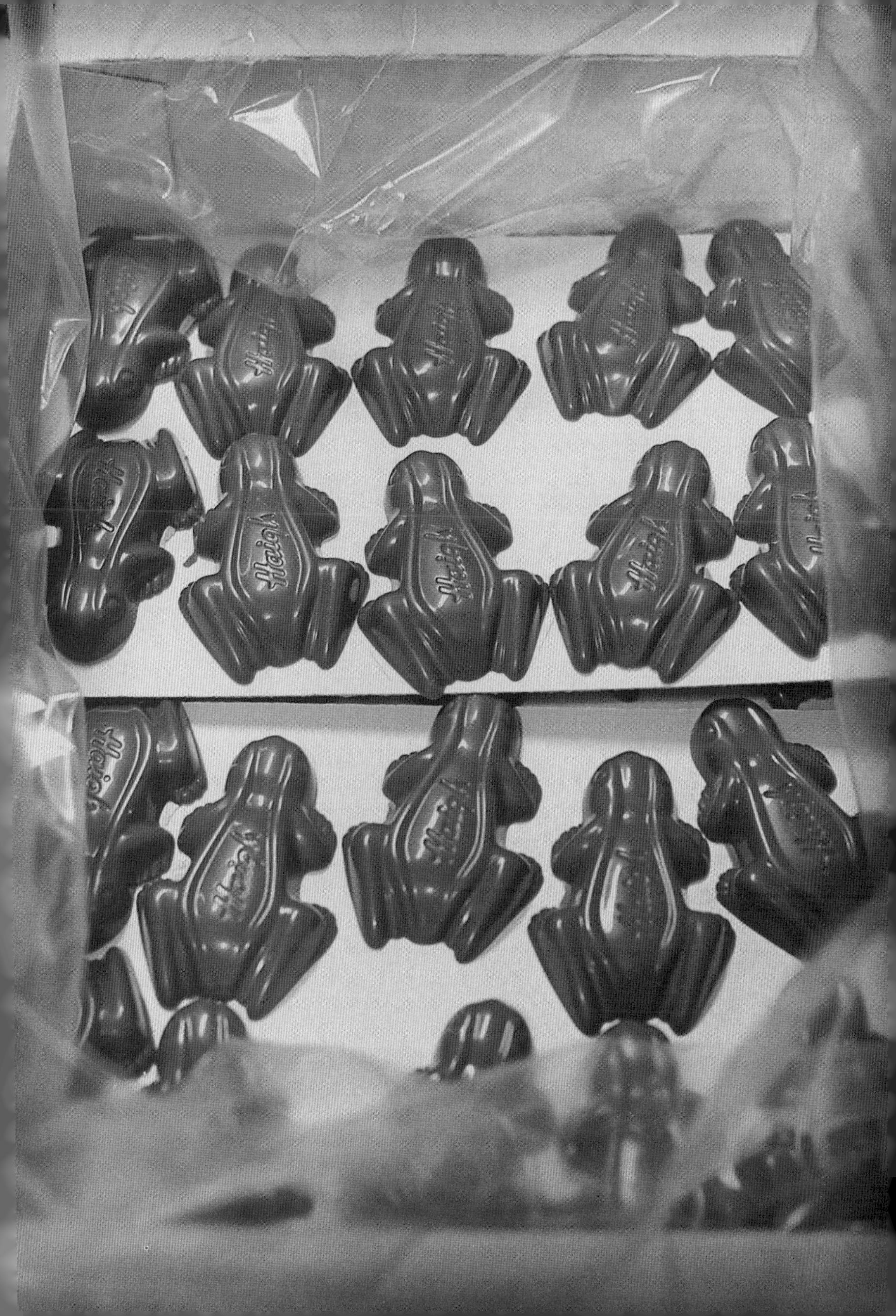
Haigh

Author's Note

I would like to thank all at Wakefield Press for their patience and support as I came to realise that their contribution to this project more than matched mine. Barbara Santich, food writer and historian, who has done this sort of thing many times before, I thank for her understanding of the process and her subtle encouragement with many snippets of information.

I also thank the following chefs who generously answered our call for recipes: Philip Johnson of écco bistro, Stephanie Alexander, Alison and Michael Voumard of the Botanic Dining Room, Nick Papazahariakis and Marc Vaca of Chloés Restaurant, Sue-Ellen Hope and Pierre Barelier of The Wild Olive Restaurant, Damien Pignolet of Bistro Moncur in the Woollahra Hotel, Paul Merrony of Merrony's Restaurant, Ann Oliver, Andrew Fielke, Justin Harmon, Barbara Santich, Patricia O'Donnell of Mietta's Queenscliff Hotel, Kelly Sugar Leonard of Juniperberry, Janni Kyritsis of MG Garage, Bill Marchetti of Marchetti's Latin, Rosa Matto, Maggie Beer and Gay Bilson. Thanks are also due to my staff at the Art Gallery Café in Adelaide, in particular Steph Heaven and Louise Naughton who tested the recipes.

Many people contributed with memories and discussion, in particular Connie Rotolo of Bottega Rotolo, and Jennifer Hillier. From overseas came valuable information from Rebecca C. Smith of Pennsylvania, Colman Andrews, author of *Catalan Cuisine*, and the performing artist and food historian Alicia Rios.

Talking with John, Alister and Simon Haigh was a delightful necessity. I particularly thank Stuart Chandler, Haigh's Marketing Manager for sharing his knowledge and for allowing me to riffle through years of accumulated wrappers.

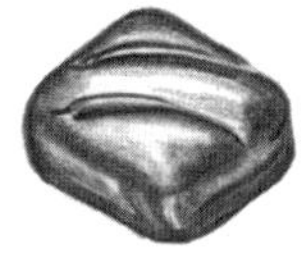

On the home front I appreciate my French mother Kiki who taught me to enjoy cooking, my English father Mike, who taught me to enjoy eating, and my brother Jean-Pierre for his fanatical love of good, natural ingredients and for making the best chocolate brownies. My partner Roger Vincent was most supportive in sharing the burden of sampling a lot of chocolate.

Photograph Captions

Photographs by Mick Bradley. Thank you to Sarah Homan, Oliver Bevan and the Haigh's staff photographed.

Bibliography

Much of the information regarding chocolate and its manufacture was gathered 'on the shop floor' of Haigh's and from talking with Simon Haigh and marketing manager Stuart Chandler who was himself a chef patissier. While this does not set out to be an encyclopedic book on the history of chocolate, I have tried to be accurate in my information and offer this bibliography as a body of reading material that is as fascinating as eating the chocolates themselves.

Andrews, Colman, *Catalan Cuisine*, Grub Street, London, 1997

Bailieux, Nathalie et al, *The Book of Chocolate*, Flammarion, Paris, 1995

Boynton, Sandra, *Chocolate, The Consuming Passion*, Methuen, London, 1982

Brillat-Savarin, Jean-Anthelme, *The Philosopher in the Kitchen*, Penguin, Harmondsworth, 1984

Coady, Chantal, *The Chocolate Companion*, Simon & Schuster, New York, 1995

Coady, Chantal, *Chocolate, the Food of the Gods*, Pavilion Books, London, 1993

Coe, Sophie & Michael, *The True History of Chocolate*, Thames & Hudson, New York, 1996

Davidson, Alan & Jane, *Dumas on Food*, Michael Joseph, London, 1975

Drummond, J.C et al, *The Englishman's Food*, Readers Union, London, 1958

Harrison, B.E et al, *The Illustrated Book of Food Plants*, Peerage Books, London, 1985

Leaver, Alex, *Making Chocolates*, Michael Joseph, London, 1975

McFadden, Christine & France, Christine, *The Ultimate Encyclopedia of Chocolate*, Lorenz Books, London, 1997

McGee, Harold, *On Food and Cooking, The Science and Lore of the Kitchen*, Allen & Unwin, Australia, 1984

Mintz, Sidney W, *Tasting Food, Tasting Freedom*, Beacon Press, Boston, 1996

Montanan, Massimo, *The Culture of Food,* Blackwell Publishers, Oxford, 1994

Petke, Slavin & Karl, Sara, *Chocolate, a Sweet Indulgence,* Chronicle Books, San Francisco, 1997

Revel, Jean-Francois, *Culture & Cuisine,* Da Capo Press, New York, 1982

Rubenstein, Helge, *The Ultimate Chocolate Cake,* Congdon & Weed, New York, 1982

Schivelbusch, Wolfgang, *Tastes of Paradise,* Pantheon, New York, 1992

Skuse, E, *Skuse's Complete Confectioner,* W.J Bush & Co, London, 1928

Stacey, Michelle, *Consumed - Why Americans Love, Hate & Fear Food,* Simon & Schuster, New York, 1984

Tannahill, Reay, *Food in History,* Crown Publishers, New York, 1988

Toussaint-Samat, Maguelonne, *A History of Food,* Blackwell Publishers, Oxford, 1992

Von Welanetz, Diana & Paul, *The Von Welanetz Guide to Ethnic Ingredients,* Warner Books, London, 1983

Wheaton, Barbara Ketcham, *Savouring the Past,* Chatto & Windus, London, 1983

Wild, Anthony, *The East India Company Book of Chocolate,* Harper Collins, London, 1995

Journal

Swift, Richard, 'The Cocoa Chain', New Internationalist, no. 304, *New Internationalist,* London, 1998

Recipe Index

Savoury Dishes

Sweet Dishes

After Dinner

Chocolate Cakes and Biscuits

Frozen Desserts

Dessert Cakes

Pots of Chocolate

Soft Centres

Tarts

The Mistress's Own

yummy